CONTENTS

Copyright	1
Preface	5
Chapter 1 - Do Your Homework	7
Chapter 2 - Which Baskets to Choose for Your Eggs?	47
Chapter 3 - Setting the Game Plan	81
Chapter 4 - All Hail the Funnels	107
Afterword	135

Copyright © 2020 Yogesh Jain

All rights reserved

The characters and events portrayed in this book are fictitious. Any similarity to real persons, living or dead, is coincidental and not intended by the author.

No part of this book may be reproduced, or stored in a retrieval system, or transmitted in any form or by any means, electronic, mechanical, photocopying, recording, or otherwise, without express written permission of the publisher.

ISBN: 9798577284657
ASIN: B08PXJZD9B

Printed in the United States of America

PREFACE

Hey Growth Hacker,

I am Yogesh, your buddy who would love to help you in your journey to becoming a kick-ass marketer. I wrote this book for marketers, entrepreneurs, and knowledge seekers who want to sell software and services through digital mediums.

In my career as a digital marketer, I experienced the industry from different viewpoints. First as a content marketer, then as an account executive, and now as a consultant and media buyer. This book is my attempt to pour in the experience and knowledge gained from working for a diverse clientele and help you avoid some mistakes I made in my journey so far.

You will find personal anecdotes, case studies, research, best practices, tips, tricks, steps, a lot of excel sheets, and visual aids to help you grasp the concepts. The book allows skim readers to jump to sections they think apply to them. Though you can start anywhere, I recommend giving this a read sequentially as we understand some concepts better when you know the background.

I would also like to include a few words about Amrutha, who has been my colleague for a year now and has helped me translate many of my ideas in this book and give it a presentable structure. Her thirst for sharing knowledge and experiences propelled her to blog, and eventually, she realized writing was her calling. She has experience in digital marketing on social media and enjoys working on ideation and concepts for new campaigns. She says capturing attention is all about relevance. And you can take her word for it!

I thank you for considering my work worth your time and investment and hope you have a wonderful learning experience.

If you have any thoughts, suggestions, or feedback please write to me at - yogesh@conceptallies.com

CHAPTER 1 - DO YOUR HOMEWORK

When I started independent consulting, I got to learn a lot from my first client. The client was in the business of IT services, primarily targeting US startups. As usual, I started working my way from the existing assets of the client. This seems like a reasonable way to begin a content marketing project, doesn't it? I delivered quite effective content for the emailers, website, and collaterals, and it turned out to be a productive first month. The head of marketing was excited as I had not only over-performed but also delivered at a pace that put things on the fast track. Hence, they could start other marketing activities like advertising and email marketing on time. I still remember the call with the company CEO when he asked me three questions:

1. Does the content differentiate us from all the other service providers who also call themselves the "best in business"?
2. We also offer services in Blockchain app development. Why is it not mentioned anywhere on our

website?
3. How do you plan to scale results organically as the niche is very competitive, and there are already many generic tech articles, like yours, on the web?

Experienced marketers think on these lines even before signing the contract, let alone starting the work. While I was aware of the best practices, the rush to deliver results got the better of me. I delivered content based on the existing market research and articles. Thus, ending up with the same jargon that is already available on the Internet. It is challenging to contrast yourself in an intangible product environment, and our content was struggling to stand out. Now that we didn't have clear answers, we went into extensive reworking which resulted in delays from expected deadlines. We eventually lost the client, but the lessons learned helped us do a better job for every client in the future. Hence, I dedicated my first chapter to the teachings from this failure. We'll see what we could have done differently by doing better research and planning, and how that would have translated into fruitful results. Let's start with the simplest and one of the most widely used customer research methods - Buyer Personas.

Buyer Persona

Knowing one's target market is critical to not just marketing but to running a successful business altogether, and Buyer Persona is one of the best tools that can help you do that. A buyer persona is a fictional representation of your target customer. It's an approach to research about your target customer in a way that covers all the essential points for marketers, product managers, and the company.

Buyer Persona has become synonymous with *HubSpot* (Marketing Automation software) for all the right reasons. With an array of tools, guides, and blogs, they have made their stand clear on knowing one's target customer. One persona is an absolute necessity, but a company can have more if they target distinctive customer profiles. A persona is powerful when it's based on data, research, and interviews.

To help you understand it better, we have made a sample buyer persona. This persona is relevant for a marketer of LinkedIn Sales Navigator. LinkedIn is the biggest professional network with a database of over 500 million professionals around the world. Sales Navigator is a tool that is used to search through LinkedIn profiles using filters like job titles, company headcount, etc. to find relevant prospects. LinkedIn charges a premium price for access to Sales Navigator and it is a successful and efficient product.

Smith the Sales Guy
Business Development Executive

Identifiers

Age:
25 to 45 years

Education
Bachelor's degree (e.g. BA, BS)

Social Networks:
LinkedIn, Facebook, Twitter

Industry
Technology

Organization Size:
51-200 Employees

Personal Profile

I am a sales specialist with a knack of finding prospects and proven experience in bringing revenue to the firm thorough it's ideal clients.

How to reach out ?

Preferred Method of Communication

- Email
- Face-To-face
- Phone

They Gain Information From

- Business Websites
- Peers
- LinkedIn

Tools They Need to Do Their Job

- CRM Software
- Productivity Tools (Like Sticky Notes)

Work Life

Job Responsibilities

- Find Prospects
- Nurture Leads
- Close Deals
- Generate Revenue

Goals

- Leads Generated
- Revenue Generated

Biggest Challenges

- Prospects Don't Engage
- Finding it hard to close deals

Reports To

- Head of Sales
- CEO
- VP Sales

How does my business address these pain points?

LinkedIn Sales Navigator contains records of millions of professionals around the world. Thus, we can help Smith find the potential customers.

Notice how by giving a name and background to the target customer, we have infused life into the research. HubSpot offers a fantastic tool to make such buyer personas and get them in a presentable form for free. You can try their persona maker tool here - https://www.hubspot.com/make-my-persona

Understanding Buyer Persona in Parts

Let's see how knowledge of each of these heads is vital for a business:

Identifiers

These are demographic and professional details about the prospect that'll enable you to target them in your marketing campaigns. These details will help you identify the right tonality, target platforms for promotions, structure pay per click campaigns, find them on social media, and more.

How to Reach Out?

This information is your marketing gold mine. With preferred methods of communication, you learn which mediums are relevant for nurturing and contacting the leads. For instance, if a person doesn't prefer text messages, it's best not to invest in SMS-based marketing activities.

The way your prospect gains information about new products informs you how to strategize your branding activities. For instance, if you are marketing a B2B product, then *LinkedIn* is a better bet than *Instagram,* so they take your solution seriously.

You can create content around the tools your prospects currently use and even plan integrations as a product manager so that your solution easily fits into your client's business process.

Work-Life/Psychographics

Your prospect's work-life helps you make the best copy for your product. Be it any channel, you must communicate how your product helps them fulfil responsibilities, resolve challenges, and achieve goals. In case your SaaS product works on the B2C model, you can tweak the work-life section into a psychographic analysis about their likes, dislikes, interests, etc. to refine your targeting and messaging.

Professional Summary

It is a brief introduction to your target customer. With the professional summary, you can project the entire persona, and bring it to life in a more relatable fashion.

How Does My Business Address These Pain Points?

Now that your persona is almost ready, it's time to connect the dots. By going through the information about the potential customer, you define how your solution helps them.

Frequently Asked Questions:

How do I collect this information for my personas?
A simple answer to that is - straight from your customers. You can schedule group interviews, surveys, or just hop on

the phone and pick their brain.

If you don't have enough customers already, or if you feel that calling them for this information is inappropriate, there are other ways to get the same information. Though Google provides answers to most of our questions, social media platforms can offer unique insights. For instance, you can use LinkedIn to research job titles and Facebook groups to understand common issues with current solutions. You can also conduct a survey or use hypothetical answers based on your experience.

When should I use this information?
A buyer persona should become the basis of all the content that your company produces. It includes blogs, emails, messages, ads, and even help-docs of your product.

How many personas should I have?
It depends on your business and industry, but at least one.

Who should use these personas?
Anyone in your organization that interacts with customers, your sales team, product managers, account managers, customer service, writers, new employees - basically everyone.

How often should I update my personas?
It depends on your industry and company size. There is no one size fits all. I would suggest to review them at least quarterly and adjust based on what suits your company. If you are in the early stage of finding the product-market fit, then you'll need more frequent reviews.

How do I make sure my team uses it?
The best way to ensure it is to involve your team in cre-

ating personas. Include your team in interviews and take their feedback on the research. Your personas should be a part of your culture. We can achieve it when we emphasize their importance often and surround ourselves with people who buy into this culture.

SWOT Analysis

SWOT is an acronym for Strength, Weakness, Opportunity, and Threat. SWOT analysis gives critical insights into different aspects of a business that serve as a basis for not just marketing but all kinds of business decisions. Once you have a SWOT analysis, understanding the angle of your content should be a piece of cake.

Each element of SWOT signifies a different aspect of a business. We will drill down further into them individually to gain a deeper understanding:

Strength:

A company's strength refers to the existing capabilities that give it an advantage in the market. These can be its proprietary technology, relationship with customers, brand value, etc. These are the benefits that a business should market and build upon to strengthen its hold in the market. As a marketer, you must hammer down these strengths in your communication and maintain these advantages over the long run. To figure out your strengths, try asking these questions:

- What are the things that your company does exceptionally well?
- Are there any qualities that separate you from your competition?
- Do you hold any technological or legal advantages like trademarks, patents, proprietary technology?

- Do you have a team that gives an edge over your competitors?
- What are your Unique Selling Propositions (USPs)?

Weakness:

Your product's weaknesses are the parameters that limit your business growth and give your competitors an advantage over you. Some examples of weakness are lack of capital, no differentiating factors in the market, higher cost of production, negative emotions around your brand, etc. We need to overcome these weaknesses over time or eventually convert them into a positive attribute using marketing. For example, we can market a higher cost of a product as an indicator of premium quality. Here are some questions that will help you identify your weaknesses:

- What are the things that your company lacks, which are available to your competitors?
- How is your competitor better than you in some aspects?
- Do you have any resource limitations like capital, talented personnel, etc.?
- Is your location limiting your access to talent and customers?
- Are you not clear about your unique selling proposition?

Opportunity:

Opportunity is everything that could help you grow your

business and profitability because of market conditions and external factors. Some examples of opportunities include - exit of competitors from the market, new government regulation to help your business, opening of a new market segment for your product, etc. Awareness about these factors will help you take advantage of them by planning your campaigns. You can ask these questions to identify new opportunities:

- Is there a market that is unexplored or underserved with a need for your product?
- Is there an emerging need for your product or service?
- Did your company gain any media attention recently?
- Is there any budget, tool, or resource that is not utilized to its full potential?
- Is any advertising channel exceeding your expectations?

Threat:

Threats are technological, social, economic, or political factors that can limit your business growth or even cause substantial losses if not dealt with correctly. A threat can be new government regulations hampering trade, entry of a strong competitor, negative publicity of your brand, etc. As efficient marketers, you need to counter threats with effective Online Reputation Management (ORM), changes in product pricing and features, etc. Here are some questions that can uncover potential risks to your business:

- Is the overall economic activity taking a downturn?
- Are there changes in consumer's lifestyles that could affect the need for your product?
- Is there a global activity (like a pandemic) that could mark a significant shift in consumerism?
- Are you non-compliant with upcoming or newly introduced statutory regulations?
- Is there a change in buyer sentiments and behavior because of emergency conditions?

While strengths and weaknesses are internal factors, opportunities, and threats are external. It takes more effort to identify and channelize external factors as they are beyond your control. You need to channelize the strength and opportunities and curtail (or nullify) the influence of weaknesses and threats. You shouldn't ignore the vulnerabilities but overcome your company's weaknesses and deal with threats to the maximum effect possible.

Case Study - Shopify

Now that we understand the concept, let's see how it can put it into practice. For understanding, let's take a product that almost everyone is familiar with, i.e., *Shopify*. The e-commerce giant has done a fantastic job of becoming the go-to platform for simplified online selling. Let's see how its SWOT analysis fits with its marketing strategy.

STRENGTHS
What are you doing well? What sets you apart? What are your good qualities?

WEAKNESSES
Where do you need to improve? Are resources adequate? What do others do better than you?

OPPORTUNITIES
What are your goals? Are demands shifting? How can it be improved?

THREATS
What are the blockers you're facing? What are factors outside of your control?

Strengths:

App and Partner Network Effects

Shopify integrates with a vast number of marketing and development solutions. Plus, it integrates well with Zapier, which increases the number of possibilities manifolds. This allows easy discovery, familiarity, and set up for *Shopify* customers, making it a flexible choice.

Large Customer Base

With over 600,000 customers and counting, *Shopify* has a community of its own that acts as product advocates and finds novel ways to leverage the solutions. If you run into a problem, then chances are that some other customer has already got a solution for you, and your answer is just a search away.

Domain Expertise

Through years of continuous training and investment in

the development of human resources, *Shopify* has built a team of highly skilled workforce. Their culture is strong enough to keep up employee morale and motivate them to achieve more.

Economic Stability

Every customer that associates with *Shopify* brings in long-term value. The inherent hassle of shifting websites from one architecture to another ensures that every customer sticks with them for the long haul. Hence, *Shopify* has reliable and robust cash flows, enabling the company to expand into new projects.

Strong Distribution Network

Shopify has not just built an enormous customer base, but also a robust distribution network. There are ample marketing agencies and technology enablers offering Shopify solutions. Reliable dealership and distribution allow them to focus on development while delegating some aspects of customer support and marketing.

Weaknesses:

Lack of Personal Touch

The company lacks a personal touch with customers, which smaller e-commerce service providers can offer. It doesn't come as a surprise, as it is a common problem with most of the tech giants. It though translates into losing some market share on small businesses as smaller competitors can offer customized pricing and account management.

Challenging Expansion in New Geographies

The firm plans to grow fast globally, but the economies, marketing, language, purchasing power, and technical maturity of each country are different. For a multinational corporation, it's difficult to expand rapidly without customizing its marketing approach, which requires massive investment in technology, marketing, customer education, and human resource development.

Product Learning Curve

Shopify came after the successful launch of many eCommerce solutions. Some of these, like *WooCommerce*, enjoy the benefit of familiarity as *WordPress* developers find it easier to learn more about the same product than learning entirely new software like *Shopify*. The learning before implementation results in losing potential customers.

Lack of Clear Differentiators

Shopify is one of the many e-commerce solutions available in the market today. With all of them offering all significant functionalities, it is challenging to differentiate *Shopify* from its competitors. It's the branding efforts of the company that enable it to stand its ground, which may not be the best way to sustain visibility in the crowded market - especially in the long run.

Problems with Employee Satisfaction

While researching the company, I realized that many forums are talking about high work pressure and attrition rate. Negative reviews about the employer hurt their potential in the job market. Potential employees may look for companies where they either have connections or are sure about an appropriate work-life balance. The company needs to work diligently with sites like *Glassdoor* to ensure that such negative reviews are minimum and employees are happy after leaving the company.

Opportunities:

Harness Massive Shift to Digital Consumption

At the time of writing this book, COVID-19 had already become a worldwide pandemic, bringing a massive spike in digital consumption. This includes shopping, entertainment, work, and communication. With a growing preference for digital content consumption and shopping, it's an excellent opportunity for *Shopify* to market extensively and grab the increasing share of the market.

Growth in Demand for Cloud-Based Services

On-Premise solutions are expensive, and open source solutions don't offer priority customer support. This has increased the demand for cloud-based solutions that charge a nominal fee for continuous support. The Software as a Service (SaaS) model has become an accepted approach to product delivery for technology companies. It is scalable, affordable, and caters to the needs of individual customers. *Shopify* can leverage this full acceptance as a plus point of its product.

Ease of Internet Access

Developing countries (like India) are working hard to bring internet connectivity to even the remote areas. As a growing digital audience translates to more consumers and e-commerce businesses, *Shopify* can tailor its offering to meet the demands of an increasing customer base in such countries.

Growth of Integrated Partners

Marketing automation has become the need for every business today. With integration and automation tools, we no longer need to sync data from different platforms manually. Many such tools, like *Zapier*, have built a massive customer base. It means customers of these platforms can choose Shopify for their e-commerce needs. All we need is a marketing strategy to leverage this trend.

Government Initiatives

Green initiatives by the government have brought ease in doing online business. There are many subsidies and tax benefits also introduced from time to time for small businesses. Developed economies have also given relaxation to firms during the pandemic. These combined enable exponential growth for e-commerce businesses and translates to more customers for Shopify.

Threats:

Regulatory and Legal Issues

Shopify functions in a global environment which requires it to comply with ever-changing laws related to data protection, privacy, customer service, etc. The ability of the top management to remain familiar with regional legalities is limited. Either the company has to invest immensely in legal or face the risk of penalties because of non-compliance.

Extremely Competitive Industry

The e-commerce industry regularly witnesses hundreds of innovative startups. It is easy for a new entrant to take away years of hard work from a company with a product that is better or available at a lower price. The company is always on edge and needs to be proactive in market research.

Declining Economy

While the COVID-19 pandemic has increased online shopping, it has also brought an overall downturn in economic activity and purchasing power with the consumers. People save resources for essentials and not to spend much on luxury goods or travel. Thus, Shopify customers will face loss resulting in the shutdown of some businesses, job losses and problems with expansion.

Globalization

For countries like India, Vietnam, China, it is easier to access human resources at a low cost, resulting in an overall lower cost of production and maintenance of software. Globalization allows such competitive software like Zoho to enter global markets and offer similar offerings at a lower price.

Exchange Rates

Shopify, being a global company, is subject to fluctuating exchange rates. It is usually not a problem, but with economic uncertainties, the company needs to minimize any potential loss from international transactions.

How it Fits

Let's see how effective use of SWOT analysis is clear from Shopify's marketing

Early Branding

Are you thinking of starting a business of your own? Voila, Shopify is there for you with a cool business name generator. The company has blog posts, courses, videos, tools for entrepreneurs, even when they are just thinking about starting a business. It lays down the groundwork for a trustworthy brand that a potential client may later explore when they begin execution. This helps them fight the battle of the noisy e-commerce market with dominance in organic branding.

Cross Branding

If I have an e-commerce platform, my strategy should be to woo people who have an online store or are planning one. Shouldn't it? Actually, no, it's not exactly right, and Shopify understands that. They have an entire section dedicated to educating young minds about e-commerce, marketing, development. It helps them ease the learning curve for the product, strengthen Shopify partners, and influence decision-makers.

Forum

Remember, we discussed 600,000 customers? Yep, Shopify plays well on this strength by creating a forum for people to discuss ideas, solutions, bugs, and more. By allowing people to connect and resolve issues, it creates a secondary source of help content and also ensures early identification of user issues.

Career Section

Shopify has a career section devoted to sharing thoughts about the company culture, values, employee experiences, and more. The company has a policy of global hiring, allowing it to meet the demand for quality talent by breaking the geographic boundaries. This, along with a renowned brand name, will enable them to fight any negative sentiment about the brand from a career perspective.

Partners Program

Shopify is a business enabler for not just e-commerce companies but also for IT companies. With a dedicated partner enablement policy, it allows rapid product distribution and helps clients get some personal touch from smaller vendors if they require it.

No Barrier to Entry

We know that there are plenty of free and open-source e-commerce solutions like WordPress and Magento. But they are not nearly as easy as Shopify. That, in fact, was the reason to make Shopify. By allowing users to sign up for a free trial, the company enables the user to experience the ease of the platform. Once a person sets up his e-commerce store, he is unlikely to take the effort to shift the entire website to some hard to handle free alternative that ultimately will cost him more because of technical difficulties.

As you can see, Shopify effectively plays well on its strengths and nullifies its weaknesses. The company raised funding of over $100 Million in 2013, ensuring that it can leverage the opportunities of the growing e-commerce market. The company's content caters to all kinds of audiences, whether they are starting an eCommerce business, expanding it, or optimizing for profitability. Thus, ensuring that they are always there for their customers and partners.

There is more than one way to leverage a SWOT analysis. Sophisticated business analysts perform a weighted SWOT analysis or even combine distinct elements like (strengths with opportunities) to come up with business strategies. Those are very effective and worth having a look at if you want to explore the topic in further detail. For a content marketer, a basic understanding suffices to make a strategy and determine the tone of content across platforms.

Competitor Analysis

Can you sell anything to anyone? If yes, heck, you are a genius! But let's assume you are like me who wants to put forward a solution and sell it to people who would actually consider it. Now that seems reasonable, all of us have done that. Finding our love interest and job are good examples, aren't they? Now let's complicate things a bit. How would you put forward your solution and make sure it stands out even when there are hundreds of alternatives available, some of which are even better than yours? That's life and also the dynamics of most industries today.

As a senior marketing consultant in a real estate marketing agency, we faced a pressing challenge. We were responsible for the launch of three projects in the same area, each from a different firm. To complicate things further, there were four other projects within 5-10 kilometers which were equally amazing.

After conducting a competitor analysis we realized that not just our own projects were competing against each other but also the competitors were targeting the same market segments. Fortunately, we had few advantages in each project:

Project A: Ample amenities and within one kilometer of the upcoming commercial hub
Project B: The lowest price in the market, with the upcoming commercial hub just a few kilometers away.
Project C: The only builder in the area who was offering smart homes with no surcharge, also just minutes away from the upcoming commercial hub.

As you can see, all our clients had projects near the upcoming commercial hub and they also had their unique advantages. The marketing budgets were sufficient to make a new project launch successful under normal circumstances. However, in this scenario, there were too many options for anyone to stand out.

After hours of discussion, we arrived at the conclusion we couldn't make this successful by running ads specific to each project's unique advantage, and the cost of advertising was extremely high with no chance of making a good return on investment. So we decided that we will not market the projects, but we'll market the location.

Thanks to our skillful designers, we could make brief clips of the experience a person would get if they live close to the upcoming commercial hub. These clips were then tailored to the brand and individual advantages of each project.

The projects were still competing with each other but their combined marketing investment ensured that the experience of living in the upcoming prime location reaches not just the target segment but the entire city. With a combination of hoardings, social media ads, and word of mouth, we turned a minor advantage into a deal maker. Although the projects catered to the same customer, their combined marketing efforts blew competitors out of the water.

An effective competitor analysis enables you to understand the market conditions and adjust your go-to-market strategy. That said, you shouldn't copy your competitors blindly because neither that will give your product any differentiating factors nor there is any certainty that your competitor is right. They might be jumping from a cliff and you may end up tagging along.

How to do a Competitor Analysis?

With so many alternative solutions available in the SaaS service model it is not advisable to spend time evaluating each of them. On top of that, you don't need your competitor's entire company history to come up with a go-to-market strategy. The key is to invest your resources optimally and the below points can help you ensure that.

Choosing the Right Competitors

Choosing the right competitors is the first and the most critical step of any efficient competitor analysis. Otherwise, you may end up spending a lot of time and effort without any actionable insights. There are two types of competitors out there whom you should consider:

1. Direct Competitors - Those who target the same customer as yours with the same or similar service/solution and for the same problem. Example - Slack vs. Microsoft Teams
2. Indirect Competitors - Those who are similar to your company but differ in a key aspect. For example, they may offer services to the same customer for the same problem but a radically different solution. For example - Slack vs. Google Hangouts

Here is a grid to simplify this with an example:

Software	Customer	Problem	Solution
Slack vs Microsoft Teams		Direct Competitor	
Slack vs Pastel	✓	While Slack is designed for multi-purpose team communication, Pastel is an app specifically for communication on web design and user feedback.	✓
Slack vs Blink	Slack and Blink both can solve the same use case but Slack is a general purpose platform for any kind of business while Blink is designed specially for remote teams.	✓	✓
Slack vs JIRA		✓	✓	Slack is an organized team communication system for fast feedbacks while JIRA helps in raising tickets and tracking formal communication.

We suggest that you look at your direct competitors and close indirect competitors to get the full picture of the market. Especially the competitors who serve the same customers. They can easily expand their offering and take your market share because they already have access to your customer base.

Things You Can Compare

Company Dynamics

Information on founding year, employee count, number of customers, and market share helps you benchmark your progress with respect to your competitor. Often a direct comparison can make you feel threatened unnecessarily. By understanding your growth rate in contrast to your competitor, you can get a fair idea of your progress.

You can also dig in about the investors, capital, and recent mergers and acquisitions of the company. These things can give you a broad picture of your competitor's growth strategy and expansion plans. If you want to perform a granular analysis of a competitor, consider a SWOT analysis to complement your competitor analysis.

Go to Market Analysis

Your competitor's approach to finding customers, selling them, and maintaining relationships makes up their go-to-market strategy. You can gain an understanding of their target customer, what messaging and platform they use, and how they sell to their customers.

Intelligence on market strategy will enable you to understand the pain points of your competitor's customers and gauge the efficiency of their go-to-market strategy. You can also pick up your strategic advantages and disadvantages by looking at their pricing, messaging, and product offerings.

Good places to gather information are your competitors' website, review websites, and social media accounts, especially LinkedIn. (Hint: You can see all the *Facebook* ads of your competitors in Facebook Ads Library.) Tools like *BuiltWith* and *Datanyze* which share names of the tools used by your competitors also come in handy.

Product Analysis

Understanding your competitor's product is imperative to your research. A rational customer is likely to perform a feature-by-feature comparison of a product at a comparable price point. There are plenty of sites like *G2 Crowd, Capterra, Software Advice, TrustRadius, GetApp, Founderkit,* and *Appbot* that offer details about SaaS products to facilitate such a comparison. Since your customer is likely to do this research, why not have a communication strategy that resolves their concerns?

With so many possible parameters of comparison, one can easily get overwhelmed with the work. Thankfully, as a marketer, it is not critical that you consider every aspect above. Depending on your job responsibilities, authority, and influence you can select those parameters that will help you with the areas you can control or impact. I always recommend going an extra mile for the client and doing this research nevertheless.

Case Study - Mailchimp

To help you understand the impact and usage of competitor analysis, we'll do one for you. Let's see how by doing this research for a popular email marketing tool - *Mailchimp* can help us with some unique marketing ideas.

	Mailchimp	Constant Contact	SendinBlue
Product Weaknesses	- User experience can overwhelm beginners - Lack of robust customer support	- Lack of effective web activity tracking - No option of split testing	- Lacks a bulk social media posting tool - No mobile app for monitoring on the go
Distinguishing Features	- Advanced segmentation based on user's actions, gender and age - Can run social media ads directly from the platform - Easy to use mobile app for monitoring - Efficient web event tracking	- Robust customer support - Clean and easy-to-use interface - Mobile app - Event management system for collecting invites	- Allows Transactional emails to be sent from the platform - Efficient web event tracking - Sleek UI - Cost-efficient for startups and mid-size companies
G2 Crowd Rating	4.3	3.9	4.6
Entry Offer	Freemium	Free Trial	Freemium
Entry Price	Free up to 2000 contacts	$20 / month for up to 500 contacts	Free for up to 2000 contacts
Estimated Cost For Startups	$304 per month for 50,000 contacts	$335 / month for 50,000 contacts	$169.00 / month for 150,000 emails with unlimited contacts

Before you read any further, try to come up with some ideas of your own that can help Mailchimp market itself better based on the above research. To understand this in detail, I suggest that you first look at the websites of each of these products.

Mailchimp - https://mailchimp.com/
Constant Contact - https://www.constantcontact.com/
Sendinblue - https://www.sendinblue.com/

Leverage Social Media Capabilities

The ability to combine social media campaigns with email marketing in a single platform is a clear advantage of Mailchimp. This information isn't that obvious for a person looking for an email marketing tool but can be a great add-on in the future. You can find more information about this on the website but isn't highlighted enough in blogs and on the homepage. There is plenty of scope here to acquire customers who find value in targeted social media campaigns.

Ecommerce Capabilities

For businesses that don't have a huge product range, setting up an e-commerce store can be a huge and unnecessary pain. Mailchimp offers options to have such functionality from the platform itself. This is something unique for email marketing software. If we combine this with the capability of launching ads from within the platform, we have got ourselves an amazing combination. The company can craft certain how-to videos and engage with influencers in this niche to turn this into a well-known growth marketing hack.

Turn it into a Forum

Mailchimp's customer support is not rated well on review sites. The company needs to invest in it for sure, but unfortunately, that might not be something under a digital marketer's control. The product has a huge number of active users and quite a number of new features coming up at a regular pace. They can create a community of their users to communicate with each other, solve problems, and come up with new growth tactics. We have already seen that Shopify pulled this one off extremely well.

As you can see in a blink of an eye, we had three potential marketing strategies ready for Mailchimp. This analysis is done by comparing some of the popular tools but there are many others in the market. The objective of this comparison is to help you understand how to do this research, and I hope that you try on your own. The information listed in this comparison is subject to change overtime hence if you want to make a purchase decision then consider doing your own analysis.

Digging Your Own Site

A lot can be learned by analyzing your own website. As a content marketing consultant of *KlearStack*, I had a hard time finding relevant keywords for the business. The software works as a digitization solution for invoices, receipts, and other business-related documents. Naturally, the awareness about such a solution in the minds of the target audience isn't high enough to find high volume keywords.

Moreover, the industry used a plethora of synonyms for the same solution - OCR, Document Scanners, ERP Document Automation - to name a few. Hence each of these terms had low search volume and still enough competition to keep us on our toes for months. To meet the lead targets month-over-month, we had to come with a solution that was dependable and required minimal effort.

This is where SEO analysis of the website comes in. Upon analysis, we figured that the past blogging efforts had helped us rank well already on some of the above terms and all we needed to do was some on-page SEO and create supporting content to bring ample traffic and leads organically.

Amidst a plethora of webpages listed on the search engines, visibility holds a pivotal value to ensure that your website performs well. To achieve the desired results, the first step is to perform an in-depth SEO analysis.

An SEO analysis helps to identify every opportunity or problem that you must address to enhance your website's potential in the search engine results pages (SERPs). SEO analysis is critical to improve site ranking, expand reach, drive traffic, and hit your business goals.

Let's discuss how you can perform a step-by-step SEO analysis and loop in your competitor's strategy in your marketing plan at the same time:

Step 1: Keyword Research

Keywords help you to get found easily in the pool of similar-looking web pages, articles, and blogs. Hence, the first step towards performing a thorough SEO analysis is identifying the keywords that your website is already ranking for.

By analyzing the monthly search volume and difficulty of keywords, you will quickly know what to focus on. There are several tools available such as MOZ, Semrush, Google Keyword Planner, and Ahrefs that can help you organize your keyword based on search volume and difficulty score.

Step 2: Identify the Top Competitors

Once you complete the list of keywords, type those terms into Google and pen down the top competitors that show up as the search results. There are chances that you will find the same site appearing multiple times. Identify such sites that rank many keywords in your niche and mark them as your competitors. There are tools available to let you determine the number of organic keyword rankings on Google.

Also, while finding the competitors, you must look for sites that match your skills and potential. For instance, comparing a large-scale venture like Amazon to a niche handicraft store would be an unfair comparison.

Step 3: Making the Strategy

After gaining an in-depth insight into your competitors and your ranking, you can develop a working strategy. Go for keywords that have high search volume, low competition score, and high relevance. You should avoid using the keywords that revolve around the sites with massive domain authority, as they are well trusted and rewarded by the search engine.

Note: Domain authority is an indicator of a site's trust score on search engines. You can find it using *Mozbar*.

Chalk out some quick sources of referral traffic and backlinks too, as this brings in the much needed initial momentum. A good starting point would be Quora, Medium, the comments section of popular blogs, etc.

Once done with the above steps, determine the number of articles you will share on your blog per week, the focus keyword of each content, length of each blog, and frequency of posts on social media.

Step 4. Check URLs and Meta Description

URLs are not just links anymore, they also affect your click-through rate, website ranking, and showcase your website structure. Hence you need to ensure that all of them are functioning properly. Check for any broken links and if you spot one, then try to redirect the user to an appropriate page. Avoid changing existing URLs as that can negatively affect your current website ranking. For any new content, keep the URLs simple, short, and relevant to the content.

> **en.wikipedia**.org › wiki › Content_marketing ▾
> **Content** marketing - Wikipedia   Meta Description
> Content marketing is a form of marketing focused on creating, publishing, and distributing content for a targeted audience online. It is often used by businesses in order to: Attract attention and generate leads. Expand their customer base. Generate or increase online sales.
> History · Implications · Common metrics · Digital use

Meta descriptions are descriptive texts that you see in the search results page. Write meta descriptions accurately to attract and engage visitors. Always use your focus keywords here to improve the click-through rates. Unfortunately, meta descriptions aren't very effective SEO elements like they used to be, but they still can affect your click-through rates.

Step 5. Evaluate Links

Incoming links or backlinks are the indicators used by search engines to label your site as a trustworthy and reliable source. These links, hyperlinked on another site, impact the SEO rankings of your site.

Analyze these links to ensure that there aren't any spammy sites linking to your website. *Ahrefs* and *SEMRush* are great in performing a backlink audit and help you find any such sites. A link from a blacklisted site can bring down your site's trust score sharply.

Step 6. Check the page loading speed

Speed can affect user experience, especially on mobile devices. Make sure that the page load speed is less than 2 sec. *Pingdom* and *Google Page Insights* can help you quickly estimate the load speed and optimize it.

Step 7. Checking heading and title tag

Your page title should catch the attention of the visitors and encourage them to visit your blog. You can improve your chances of ranking by including keywords in headings and title. Always try to inculcate a long tail keyword to enhance your chances to show up on top in search results.

Step 8. Image alt text and image size

Optimize your images with proper alt text that describes the appearance and function of that image. Also, consider the image size before uploading it. As media size contributes to the page load speed, compress the images to minimize their impact. *ImageOptim* is one such tool that can help you perform this step.

Step 9. Bounce rates

Bounce rates determine the percentage of users who visit your site and leave without visiting any other page. It depicts the single engagement visits and hence is an important factor to optimize not just for search engine optimization but for your overall marketing.

It does not depict the time a user spends on your webpage, but marketers often interpret this rate to determine whether the viewer got the solution he was looking for on your page. To fix the bounce rates, check the loading speed of the page, quality of the content, design, the mismatch between content and keywords, and poor mobile optimization. Fixing your bounce rate can also improve your

SERP ranking.

SEO analysis provides you with an in-depth insight on how to enhance the website's ranking on various search engines. With an accurate SEO analysis, you can figure out the factors that are benefiting you and the aspects you need to work on to improve the site rankings. These steps will help you make strategic decisions to expand your reach and drive traffic to the website.

Keyword Research

While doing an SEO analysis helps you find the low hanging fruits, you'll still need complimentary keyword research to find new areas of growth. Here is an approach that worked well for me:

Step 1: Pen down the essential topics that apply to your business

Make a list of the topics that apply to your products or services. Now write the sub-topics for each of these categories, and you will end up having almost 10 - 12 broad categories. These topics will be enough to contain all that you want to tell your target audience.

For instance, if your company sells email marketing software, the most general topic buckets will be:

"inbound marketing" (21K)
"blogging" (19K)
"email marketing" (30K)
"lead generation" (17K)
"marketing automation" (8.5K)

The numbers written alongside these terms are the monthly search volume (representative figures). This data will allow you to analyze the topics that your audience looks out for. You can create content around these generic topic buckets with different sub-topics.

Step 2: Pamper the topic buckets with keywords

Now that you know about the topic buckets, you can now look for the keywords crucial to rank in the search engine result pages. Workaround the topic buckets that you have created and think of the most common keyword phrases that people would have searched for (related to that topic).

If you are brainstorming around "marketing automation," the most common search phrases can be the questions around the topic. For instance - What is marketing automation? What are the tools for marketing automation? How is marketing automation software useful? How to use marketing automation tools? Why do we need marketing automation for business? What are the top automation tools? And so on. Answer the Public is an amazing tool for this purpose.

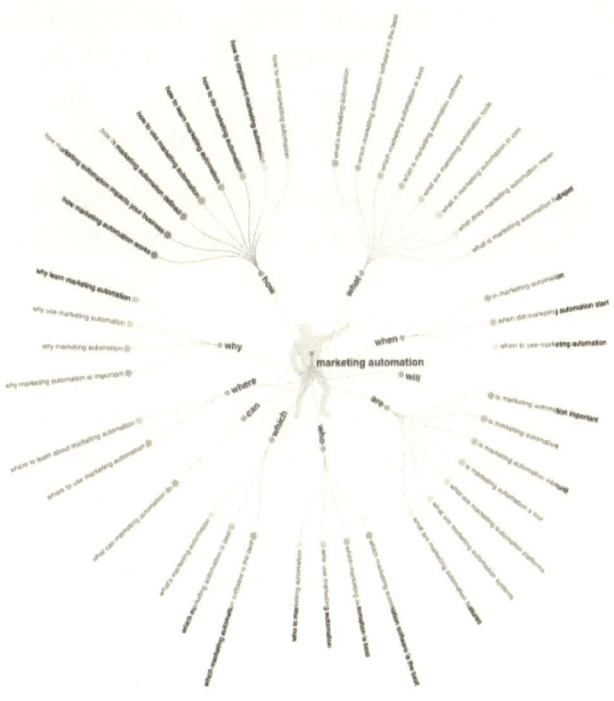

You can also look for keywords that are already helping your website appear in the search engine by using Google Search Console and write more on the keywords that apply to your business. Another way of finding customer's pain points is to interview them through direct emails or surveys.

Once you make this list, you can highlight the topics frequently discussed in the sales conversation, to help generate quality leads.

Step 3: Understand How Intent Can Impact Keyword Research and Strategize Accordingly

Address the intent of the user before writing content. We all search for different topics every day, and we realize that Google doesn't always address our intent in the search result. Therefore, it becomes important to find and fill these gaps than just writing keyword-stuffed content.

Keywords are a pivotal way to be found on the web, but a keyword might mean differently to every individual. To identify the intent behind a search, it is essential to interpret the keywords that you use.

Let's say if you are researching "how to use social media to create an impact" to write an article. The topic is vast and can have many interpretations. While you can provide tips for every social media platform, "impact" here can mean generating revenue for the business or becoming a social media influencer. Having a sense of intent will lead the direction of your article.

To know the user's intent in a keyword, you can put these keywords in the browser and look for the first few results.

These are the ones that are consistently meeting the user's intent, and hence you'll get a rough idea behind the search.

Step 4: Target related search terms

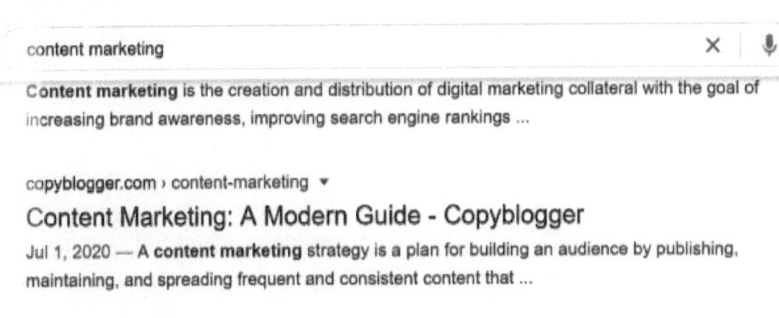

This is a necessary step many of you are already performing while doing keyword research. If you are not doing this, it's a great way to start. If you cannot think of more keywords about any specific topic, you can always rely on the related search terms that you find when you search for the keyword in the search engine.

Step 5: Take the help of keyword research tools

There is plenty of keyword research and SEO tools that help find keywords based on the topics you want to write about. To name a few, *Ahrefs, SEMrush,* and *Ubersuggest* let you find the exact match keywords and phrases for your content strategy. After performing the required research, you can give these tools a try to get more alternatives and data like search volume and difficulty score on each keyword.

Ensure that you re-evaluate these keywords every couple of months to stay relevant. When you gain considerable authority, you can add more broad keywords to your lists but if you are just starting, then focus on longer keywords with lower competition.

CHAPTER 2 - WHICH BASKETS TO CHOOSE FOR YOUR EGGS?

In a world that has bought into the "Netflix and Chill" ideology, where content is consumed on-demand, with focus placed on specific events and mood, it feels like there's nothing more you can do.

Just when you think "been there, done that" you discover something more. In the next few chapters, I aim at breaking the stereotypes for social media channels and their use for content marketing.

Social media is a powerful tool for those who know how the reactor core and its components work. Though it sounds like something that exists since the invention of TV, advertising your product is still very much relevant and needed.

See humans respond to the stimulus of an ad like a happy

family, a favorite celebrity, or glossy lifestyles. And that very response is what we need to capture in our marketing content.

Online content marketing is the future and the present. We are all very comfortable going digital, and with more people spending time on hand-held devices, our content marketing strategies should also change accordingly.

But what does that mean exactly? Let's take an example of a daily use product like hair gel. Conventionally, the marketing strategy behind promoting or advertising hair products was to hire a model with the most luscious locks and enhance their looks.

Today, however, people don't want to conform to one kind of beauty standard, and that's where the marketing strategy comes in. Imagine you set a premise or tell a story behind how you create the hair gel, maybe even go into the roots of the ingredients. When your audience is more aware or in other terms enlightened about the hair gel, they are more likely to prefer your brand over your competitors.

So before you launch a new line of hair gels, you have created a need for that product via content marketing online.

Videos and graphical representations of these products are also key when setting a premise. No one wants to read about the goodness, they want to see it in action. What that means is to show the audience the inner-mechanisms of the product, almost.

We can see this type of content marketing on many social media channels, especially Instagram. *Dior*, the French luxury fashion house, has been very successful in reaching out to its target audience better by uploading snippets on how they manufacture their products. In a series of posts, they upload small clips of making either a shoe or a bag, starting with its sketch, showing the stitching and polishing process, and finally doing finishing touches. This makes the audience feel like they were a part of that product's odyssey and almost feel loyal towards it.

And with *Instagram* providing every tool needed to make better conversions, many other brands are leading the audience to their websites with more success.

It's all about giving out the details in small doses, building it up for the final reveal.

Here you can see how *Dior* uploaded a start to finish the journey of their product. This means the audience is already aware of recent improvements every day, increasing their curiosity about the end product.

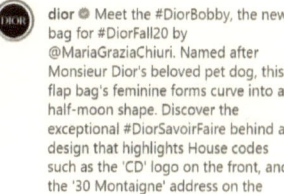

Link to Post - https://www.instagram.com/p/CCvFkLrIO7i/?utm_source=ig_web_copy_link

We know the *Bodyshop* far and wide for its ethical and conscious sourcing; and they weave that concept into their marketing strategy. Here you can see how they have isolated shea butter products by showing us the women who work on the plantations to harvest the seeds. This creates a sense of belonging to the brand's ideologies, and when you want to buy a shea butter product, you immediately think of the contributions you would make towards the women if you buy from *The Bodyshop*.

thebodyshop ⊙ "What makes me most proud is the satisfaction of the work I'm doing and the empowerment of the Tungteiya women. They are able to transact business on their own" – Madame Monica.

Thank you for your continued support in helping us economically empower people all over the world. Through purchasing our shea products, you are supporting the Tungteiya Women's Association in Ghana, where we've been sustainably sourcing our shea butter from since 1994. This programme helps to empower 640 women, allowing them to achieve an independent income and help fund community projects.

Link to Post - https://www.instagram.com/p/CBOH8FRHQGF/?utm_source=ig_web_copy_link

Choosing the Right Social Channels

Content marketing is basically good storytelling. You need to hook your audience to the journey of the hero (the product in question) and get them invested to know more about the long and short of it.

While we are all aware of the wonders strategically placed website ads can do to a product's success, we mustn't underestimate social media for revenue. These user-friendly interfaces are built for a visual ride, and can give your brand a powerful lift.

Popular social media platforms like *Instagram*, *Twitter*, *Facebook*, and *YouTube* show good conversions. However, there are other platforms or apps like *TikTok*, *Spotify*, and *Snapchat* that have also proven to be influential.

Content consumption via audio streaming apps and services like *Apple Podcasts* and *Spotify* have also increased over the years, and although they are not very marketing-friendly, some companies have found ways to advertise themselves or push content on these platforms too through their influencers.

Let's explore the nuances of these platforms, starting with *Instagram*. It is a hotbed for promotions for almost every business under the sun and here pictures speak a thousand words; literally.

As an avid user myself, with regular and business accounts on the app, I can say that Instagram has that quirky charm that gets you hooked. For users who treat it as just another digital photo album, it has a cool interface with helpful tools and photo enhancers. But for those who want to do some serious marketing through the app; you are in for a superb experience. The app is perfect for targeting young audiences with creative promotions that ultimately result in increased revenue.

Business accounts and profiles can benefit sheerly from the number of users. *Instagram* has well over 500 million users worldwide and counting. Ever since it was bought by and merged with the app world's big boss *Facebook*, it has become like an extended family to the FB tree, making it a more lucrative place for businesses to market themselves in the most creative methods.

Here's a quick look at the pros and cons of marketing your content on different social channels:

Instagram

Ideal for: Instant mass attention especially from young audiences

Pros	Cons
Post creation and freedom of content choice	Not very popular among people above 40 years of age
Ease of managing an account	Needs very interactive campaigns to become popular
Analytics at your	Limited options for

fingertips	presentation
New features/developments added regularly	May not fit into every budget

What you can do to overcome the disadvantages:

Widen your target audience by turning on the *Publish on Facebook* option. This way you can reach more people even if they don't use *Instagram*.

Facebook

Ideal for: Reaching a global audience with strong campaigns

Pros	Cons
Gain popularity and followers rapidly	Needs specific and targeted campaigns to work
Direct traffic to website more effectively	Inconsistent updates might lead to lower ranks
In-depth analysis and tools to help promote your name	Reaches only those who liked your page or are aware of your account
The most popular app in the world, with *Instagram* and *Whatsapp*, integrated into the main app	Need to invest in advertising to reach people even if they have already liked your page.

What you can do to overcome the disadvantages: The more consistent your uploads are, the more attention your account gets and you can use the same engagement in remarketing ad campaigns.

YouTube

Ideal for: Interactive video campaigns

Pros	Cons
More content consumption with regards to the length of an upload	Content sensitive. High restrictions on what you upload with the risk of being taken down
Ads can be created to appear before and during a video upload, but are skippable after the first 5 seconds.	Highly competitive. You need genuinely original content to survive
First one minute of the video hooks people in which means if your content catches the attention right from the get-go, you are more likely to succeed and gain subscribers	Open to the world, which means your work can easily be plagiarized

SELLING THROUGH CONTENT

Ample room for storytelling and even new channels can expect to get traffic, unlike the case with Google search.	Ads placed into your content might constrict your campaign

What you can do to overcome the disadvantages: To rise above the competition, make sure your content engages the user early on.

LinkedIn

Ideal for: Professional presentation of your company

Pros	Cons
High search engine visibility	Needs to be learned. Not very user friendly
Used by senior executives	Responses can be colder than other platforms
Superb recommendation algorithms	Limited presentation options
You can tag executives and comment on their posts very easily.	Can get more expensive to use all features

What you can do to overcome the disadvantages: Create interesting and original content tailored to the professional audience and use videos often.

Social Media Marketing Tools

In this ocean of data that gets shared and re-shared every second, how do you keep track of where you are and what your next plan of action should be?

Just like you have planners and trackers for everything else, content marketing on digital platforms also needs to be organized, measured, and analyzed. With the help of some advanced analytics tools, you would save a tonne of work that involves revisiting concepts, changes, and posts on each platform. And these analytics are made accessible by a buffet table full of digital marketing tools. Some are even available for free!

From keeping track of the number of likes and comments to understanding how many users are interacting with your content, digital marketing tools show us the behind-the-scenes action. These tools not only help with basic analytics, but they also point us towards our next successful move.

According to *Instagram*, 90% of its users follow at least one business that has a constant presence on the app. That means there's a potential to reach out to a high volume of people, quickly and easily.

Like with anything else, guessing games are always a gamble and it's better to know A to Z of how your content is faring online. Whether your campaigns become a hit or they bomb, there's always room for creating better strategies and with digital marketing tools like *Sprout Social* and *Hootsuite*, you will reach your audiences better.

From strategizing for email marketing, website analytics,

and customer reviews to search engine optimization and paid social media marketing, there is a need for a clearer picture of where you stand.

Did you know that there are over 30.7 million small-scale businesses in the USA alone? It's critical to understand the growing number of businesses and the number of people making those businesses digital.

Content marketing has everything to do with piquing interest in your products and services, as opposed to simply presenting a product and asking people to buy it.

Digital marketing tools can tell us details about demographics, interests, the number of impressions on a post, trending topics, segment of users interacting with us constantly, and even user behavior. You can then prioritize and come up with plans that have more success rates when compared with plans made with basic knowledge.

Some of the best tools for social media available out there are *Sprout Social, Buffer, Hootsuite,* and *Social Blade*. The analytical capabilities of these tools are advanced enough to gather information from across the globe and categorize them into different and relevant sections for an easier approach.

So really, what you get when you post using these tools is effortlessness. You can analyze all your posts (*Facebook, Instagram, Twitter,* and more) within one user-friendly dashboard where everything is visual.

You can even schedule the publishing of your upcoming posts beforehand and focus on more important things.

Content Marketing Checklist

Here is a checklist that you can use when starting with content marketing on any medium:

1. Create a reasonable budget

According to research small to medium-sized companies spend somewhere between $2500 to $12,000 per month for digital marketing campaigns. However, we don't always have a surplus of finances to shovel into our marketing strategies, so it's best to ration your budget and make the best use of every penny spent.

Three ways you can be prudent with your marketing budget:

> A. Ensure you use your tools to understand your audience and their behavior towards your business. This will help you choose the right channel and method you want to use for your digital marketing campaigns, and spend only where you are certain you will see successful conversions.
> B. Create a master template of must-have parameters for your marketing strategy and use that template as a guideline every time you want to change your approach. When you already have a framework of sorts chalked out in front of you, you'll never go over budget.
> C. Cut costs by hiring freelance professionals for content creation and begin small with wallet-friendly promotional activities on *Facebook* or *Google*. By starting small, you can learn about reactions and impressions of your audience, but should the campaign fail,

you know you haven't done much damage to your budget.

2. **Keep an eye out for trending opportunities**

   The world works on trends, and those who make the most of the opportunity can benefit enormously. Invest some time in trend forecasting and understand how the system functions.

   Channels like Twitter can give you an inside look into what's upcoming and how you can use the trends in your favour. You should also monitor your peers and industry influencers to catch upcoming trends.

3. **Take your audience seriously**

   Your audience is your best critic and judge. For most of it, anyway. You reach out to them and their response propels you further. So meet all feedback with an open mind.

   Digital platform users can be very fickle-minded, and there is no need to put everything you come across into your notes, but being present and responsive is good. Use your tools and keep that communication path open as a two-way street, you never know where your inspiration comes from.

4. **Consider the advancements in tech**

With Artificial Intelligence quickly taking a role in many parts of our daily life, a future where marketing will also have AI support is not distant.

According to ContentMarketingInstitute.com predictive time-series forecasting involving AI, mathematics and statistics will be the next big thing in the digital marketing world for analyzing brands. Text mining, data science, and probability will become the cornerstones of every marketing strategy, and though you don't need technical knowledge about how they work, you need to know the basics to understand your position. Plus, it's never a waste of time if you're learning something new! You can check out tools like IBM Watson Analytics for Social Media that already done commendable work in this field. This tool allows you to monitor your brand mentions across platforms and do a sentiment analysis so you can immediately find websites and posts that are mentioning your brand in negative light and counter accordingly.

Role of Videos in Content Marketing

What is the most important part of modern digital marketing? The simple answer to that is *user engagement*. According to a research website, a human spends an average of 2 hours and 22 minutes on the Internet per day. This means we consume content in some form or the other constantly, and businesses see this as a golden opportunity.

Television and radio have become something of the past after the introduction of other platforms designed for a richer content consumption experience. For example, snappy video marketing.

Visual representation of a product increases its value and generates engagement much more efficiently than text formats. And when it is packaged inside a brief but educative video format, users respond with positivity. While there have been TV ads for marketing professionals to create brand magic, there's something more attractive about content marketing that involves telling a customized story about your product or service via videos on digital platforms.

A product that is seen in action connects more with users as compared to something that is static or follows a more static form of communication, like pictorial representation. As per *HubSpot's* study, 85% of businesses prefer video as a marketing tool. 88% of video marketers have seen an increase in ROI of 5% and we expect it to double shortly.

Video content reaches a wider audience from all walks of life and also encourages sharing. Big names like *LEGO* and *Disney* have been engaging their viewers by cleverly using content marketing strategies within their videos.

Let's take *LEGO* as an example. From tutorials on how to build a particular *LEGO* toy, to promoting new toys released for a season-specific event, they have created content for everyone to watch and enjoy while learning.

A holiday-themed video released back in 2012, shows the perfect use of content marketing and promotions while keeping engagement at its highest.

They have not only ensured that users get a good look at the latest holiday-themed toy, but they are also encouraging viewers to share the video to spread the joy/learn how to build the new toy.

Videos that promote shopping can increase revenue to a great extent. Whatever the product, a snippy video will get the full attention and more brand recall of the viewers.

Creative directors and ad creators can say with conviction

that more and more marketing teams reach out for video formats that can be shared over various mediums like email and website links.

Today, 2D and 3D animated videos wear the crown and rule all the digital marketing strategies. A quick about us, narrated by the mascot of the business, or a beautiful story told by using some eye-catching transitions, bring about professionalism to the business.

Hosting videos showcasing a business and its operations has become a must today, as people who want to know more don't show the patience to sit through lengthy paragraphs.

What should and shouldn't be a part of your social media marketing video:

Go for these:

- A must-have while marketing via videos is a story. Unless you are showing/tutoring the audience about some technical aspects of a product, it is essential the video follows a storyline and is executed keeping in mind all the elements that make the brand/business what they are.
- Ensure you have a great execution team behind the project, and they understand the pulse of your audience and what they might respond to.
- While marketing your business/product via animated videos, make sure the visual elements are in tune with your brand and its values.
- Finish with a strong call-to-action so your audience knows exactly what to do once they watch

the video.

Ditch these:

- Run-of-the-mill narratives give the impression that you didn't take any effort into creating a tailored video.
- Robotic voice-overs and incomprehensible language might sabotage the entire campaign.
- Stuffing the video with keywords and repeating phrases can make it boring hence, keep your sales pitch minimal.
- Long and tiring lengths, where the audience is being dragged through unwanted information. There's nothing worse than video content with more fluff and less relevance. Videos like these tend to be skipped, dooming the marketing strategy altogether.

YouTube

One of the powerful digital social media platforms is the 2005-launched application, *YouTube*. The app has had a positive impact on global audiences and it only seems to grow with every new quarter.

YouTube was created by three former *PayPal* employees when they couldn't find videos of Janet Jackson's wardrobe malfunction and the Indian Ocean Tsunami disaster back in 2004.

This led to a brainstorming session, and the trio came up with an idea of wanting to create an online dating platform where they would ask people to upload their videos for some money.

Soon they found it difficult to amass such videos and dropped the dating site idea before moving on to creating what *YouTube* we know today.

The company which celebrated its 15th anniversary in 2020, became a worldwide sensation, especially to those who had all that content to share but never found the right platform.

Google was quick to pick up this framework and give it a good old transformation. *YouTube* was able to grow as they had infrastructural as well as manpower support from *Google*.

Today, from music videos and movie trailers to tutorials and even live streaming, YouTube has over 1 billion users, 103 million subscribers, and well over 6.5 billion streams.

We can say that 300 hours of footage is uploaded to *YouTube* every year.

According to research, *YouTube* alone generated $15.5 million in global advertising revenues, which accounted for 9.4% of *Google's* 2019 total annual revenue.

The site has seen a drastic change in the way it is being used today as compared to when it was a newbie. *YouTube* users are becoming more creative, and *Fortune 500* companies have tapped into the part of *YouTube* that has proven to be content marketing gold.

The competition is getting tough and there are more and more marketing experts taking things to the next level, especially with the addition of ads before and during the videos watched on YouTube.

The million-dollar question is, how to be successful at content marketing on *YouTube*?

I think for anything to be a success; you have to stick to the correct way of doing it.

YouTube Best Practices 101:

Whether your strategy involves promoting content by telling a story or you choose to create power-packed campaigns, following these guidelines will help you build a stronger foundation for a more successful video.

1. Keep your posts consistent:

You don't want to flood your subscribers' notifications with your content, but a steady flow of uploads is sure to improve your popularity.

Currently, Indian Music and Video company *T-Series* has the highest number of subscribers, clocking in at 147 million. Following close is Swedish entertainer *PewDiePie* who is known for butting heads with *T-Series*, with 106 million subscribers.

Both the *YouTube* channels show a steady pace of content shared weekly, with customized promotional previews and activities for some of their best videos.

Interaction with the audience comes down to the online patterns they follow. They will respond better to you when they can rely on your routine.

This also calls for communicating with them about when you might upload the next video. Tell your audience to watch out for a new video in the upcoming week, or if you aren't posting for a while, tell them you'll be back after a short sabbatical. This little piece of information will make your audience feel one with your account and urge them to look forward to your content.

2. Set a strong call to action

There's nothing worse than investing time and watching a video, only to feel lost about what to do with it once done. So even if you told the best story and created the most engaging content, a missing CTA will only lead to a failed campaign. Even a weak CTA can do damage, so make sure you don't hang your audience out to dry at the end of the video.

3. Expand your content goals

We all want to create exciting and shareable content. But imagine a YouTube account that only posts one kind of video. The audience is fickle and moods change according to many external factors. And though we cannot cater to all those moods, we can offer options to choose from. And that means switching your regular strategy with trending topics or even seasons.

YouTube lets you create playlists with your content, and you can use that to your advantage by categorizing your videos.

4. Get into the nooks and crannies

73% of people would positively buy a product if they have seen a video showcasing it and its features.

People want to see how a product works, or what

extra service can provide. And they will prefer videos that get into the details. Whether you want to showcase parts of your products through 2D and 3D mediums or you want to market service by showing its needs and effects, descriptive videos give you a better chance of retaining your audience's attention and gaining a new audience.

5. Ensure professionalism

While there is no bar on creativity, maintain a certain decorum. With all that commotion caused by millions of users and millions of videos, you can stand out by presenting your content by focusing on professionalism.

Sloppy work shows. Make sure you are putting your best foot forward, even if that means you have to invest in quality equipment and involve a good editing team. By doing so, you are ensuring consistency in your quality and you're already making headway in improving the brand value.

Blogging and Its Myriad Faces

I would like to think that bloggers are the Picassos and DaVincis of the digital word world because they can create words into everlasting masterpieces. It is 2020, and blogging seems like it's on the verge of facing the Dodo bird's fate. That said, blogs are still very relevant today. Did you know that websites that contain blogs have 434% more indexed pages, which helps make for an effective SEO and improves the rankings on Google and other search engines?

According to the *Hosting Tribunal*, over 77% of Internet users read blogs. Leading blogging platforms like *BlogSpot*, *WordPress*, *Medium* and *Tumblr* are hosts for over 60 million blogs and constant digital footfall. Mobile devices have also allowed blogging to stay alive with more and more users browsing and reading blogs right from their phones and tablets.

A well-worded and informative blog intrigues most readers. Owe it to the power of imagination. Just like how a book has way more grip over your mind than a film, a blog that gets your imagination running does wonders to improve your brand image online.

Whether it is a personal blog, that's like an intimate diary meant for the public eye or a piece of well-recorded firsthand information carefully curated in sets of texts, we know that journalists, bakers, astronauts, fishermen, businessmen, cyclists, basically people from all walks of life, have a platform to express themselves through exclusive stories and experiences.

So are blogs only meant to talk about personal experiences? Absolutely not! Every company wants to tell their story, share updates, and report their progress in the most creative way possible.

And blogs are the perfect way to present your company, not only to the people who are associated with you but also to potential clients and keen eyes who want to know the inner-mechanisms of your business. Most blogs nowadays are tailor made for businesses that showcase their best work, awards, progress, and even their employee engagement.

But how does one go about creating a blog that is effective and not too long to read?

Blogging Best Practices 101

The million-dollar question here is, how to write an engaging blog? While there is no cookie-cutter approach to writing a successful blog, an efficient blog surely follows the below guidelines:

1. **An informative but catchy headline**

    While keywords are very important to a blog for its ranking on search results, the title mustn't be stuffed with keywords and only keywords. A title of that nature not only looks unprofessional (clickbait), but it also confuses the readers - what the topic is.

2. **An introduction that is relevant and brief**

Blogs with introductions that ramble on forever will make the reader lose interest in the rest of the blog and also instill a feeling that the blog may not be what they are looking for. A smart and tailored introduction keeps the readers hooked and wanting for more.

3. A body that contains vital information on the main topic

The body of the blog is like the heart of the digital article. This is what the reader reads and needs to be explanatory and detailed. Just get right into it. There is no use in beating around the bush in this section. Talk about everything you want to convey, while still maintaining brevity and relevance.

4. Additional information like statistics, numbers and reports

Nothing is better than claims supported by figures and facts. Reveal all the numbers present those statistics proudly and give your reader the latest updates on your company in this section. Don't hold back with visual representation; it can have a more positive impact on reader engagement.

5. A conclusion that not only summarizes the topic but also provides a teaser.

A conclusion is as important as the body or the statistics. This is not a section just meant for summarizing what you have talked about, but a perfect space to inform your readers to keep their eyes peeled for the next move your company is about to make. It's also space where you can influence a reader to come back to your blog page or click on another related blog for additional information.

A minor note on word count:

Most professional blogs are meant for a quick read about any recent updates of the business and rarely exceed 700 words. If you have a detailed blog topic, just spread it across multiple blog topics; that way you are not overloading the readers with exhausting information.

Some SaaS Businesses Who Have Done it Right

Salesforce - YouTube

Challenge: Creating Interactive Marketing Bits

Salesforce is the most popular customer relationship management (CRM) service available in the market. And even though their product speaks for them, the company's marketing team has made sure they show a solid digital presence, especially on YouTube.

The marketing gurus at *Salesforce* have made it their motto to create outreach plans on their *YouTube* channel to keep their users (and potential users) up to date about the latest developments.

The *YouTube* channel boasts over 30 million views, 148k subscribers, and hundreds of clients, platform users, and marketing/sales execs who are happy to click on that play button as soon as they upload a new video.

Implementing Strategies that Work: Interactive Content for everyone, not just users/employees

A traditional SaaS platform would have used a social media tool like *YouTube* for just demos and basic know-how videos. But *Salesforce* has cleverly designed video content that branches further out with the sole purpose of client representation.

They maintain the same narrative on their website as well. They want us to see them as a company that is growing with the businesses of their clients. They are current, relevant, and on-point without that pesky element of the bore. They use creative infographics, catchy descriptions about their features, and don't shy away from total sensory interaction.

Sure they have how-to and demo videos across the channel, but they gain more attention because of their videos where they have a tête-à-tête with CEO's, Managers, Marketing Executives, and even the occasional celeb collaboration, through their programs like B-Well Together, and Lead Through Change. Every video touches a different, prevailing, or trending topic. They are syncing current events to their platform and by doing so they are giving their users/viewers a stage to take part in the developments the company is trying to market.

Conclusion: Staying relevant in an era where trends change ever so quickly

Social media channels, where content suits the interests of the viewers, are more successful and ensure a continued reception of interest from the audience while helping rope in new audiences.

Adobe - Instagram

Challenge: Attracting artists, designers, and art connoisseurs

The marketing and document management mega-company got one thing right when marketing themselves on social media—eye-catching posts. *Instagram* especially, thrives on quality pictures/posts, and engaging content that is curated for the app's format.

Adobe has a range of products, from the infamous *Photoshop* to their document readers like PDF. And what better way to market these products than promoting artists using these products. That's exactly what *Adobe* has cashed in on.

Implementing Strategies that Work: Inclusion and Representation

Apart from posting content that created by their in-house artists, they are tagging and sharing the art of their users. This helps pull the attention of the user's followers to their platform, and serve as a stage that showcases talent.

Besides, *Adobe* has also dedicated different *Instagram* accounts for their different platforms where they do some targeted marketing. Take their *Adobe Photoshop Lightroom* account for instance. They are committed to post everything *Lightroom*, including videos showing how to use the tool. The cleverest part about their marketing campaign is that they are not doing all the work. They are using the work of the artists to rely on their tools, to help build an image of the brand.

Instagram lives and breaths trends, and of course *Adobe* has also jumped on that train. They raise awareness, help educate followers on the current events, and even call on them to participate in their in-house programs like *Adobe* Rising Stars of Photography and WomenCreateWednesday. For further engagement, *Adobe* introduces their artists, illustrators, graphic designers, and creators as part of their CoCreate program, which brings artists from around the world, to one social media platform that helps them build their future.

This strategy has helped them gain over 1 million followers and countless reshares likes, and interactions.

Conclusion: Combine marketing strategy with empowerment

Your company is important, yes, but when it comes to digital marketing, the consumer becomes bigger than any agenda your business might have. And including them in your campaigns will only make your company more popular.

Slack - LinkedIn

Challenge: Creating a marketing strategy that convinces all working professionals that a faster communication

tool has finally arrived

Who hasn't heard of *Slack*! And a big reason why the platform is so well known even though it is meant for teams and collaborations in the business world, is their exhaustive marketing campaign.

Slack is a SaaS platform that provides an environment for all team members of the office to come together and communicate without all the chaos.

In a 2020 interview with *The Verge*, CEO Stewart Butterfield explained what *Slack* is meant for when he said, "Channel-based messaging platforms like *Slack* genuinely make life a lot easier because you join the team—you know, people started [working] at *Slack* yesterday. And there's, I don't even know, 15 million messages in the archive that are available for them to search. For their team that they work with most closely, they can scroll back over the last couple of weeks of conversations and see, not only the facts and projects that people are working on, but also how people relate to one another, what the sense of humor is, and all that stuff."

Implementing Strategies that Work: Upbeat marketing draws budding businesses

Slack is targeting businesses of the millennial era. So obviously they will aggressively use social media channels like Facebook and LinkedIn to help build their name. And what's a better platform than LinkedIn to catch the attention of professionals who are constantly looking for solutions to bridge communication gaps?

Slack manages a very successful page on *LinkedIn* with many people liking and sharing the content. They promote their brand via testimonials by head honchos of various companies who talk about current situations and how *Slack* helps them power through it all. The nifty video feature on *LinkedIn* makes their page more educative and interactive all while promoting new features and tutorials.

Slack is heavily reliant on quirky and abstract infographics for all their promotional content. From the design of their website to the videos they create for promoting their name using current trends, the platform is pushing more and more young people to take interest in what they have to offer. They have community hashtags like #slacklife used by professionals globally to show how they are using the platform or how their workplace has changed because of *Slack*.

Slack is also especially promoting their blog articles on *LinkedIn* and those 5-minute reads not just help them drive traffic to their website, but increase their popularity in the professional community, who have something valuable to say.

Conclusion: Targeted marketing plans yield better results

Companies like *Slack* that design products for a modern-day business, create up-to-the-minute marketing strategies that cater to a niche audience, rather than the market as a whole. By getting on board with the latest trends like hashtags and short vine-like videos, any business can make their presence felt in an instant.

HubSpot - Blogging

Challenge: Promoting fast-paced reading, while providing all the relevant information

Blog marketing is all about keywords and getting internet users to visit your website the most.
Who knows this better than *HubSpot*? A company that started as a SaaS platform to help other businesses build better marketing strategies, is now known for their blog marketing around the world.

Yes, blogging has taken a back seat as compared to other digital marketing methods, mostly because of the time it takes for a person to sit through a blog article. But *HubSpot* has stayed current and roped in more clients via their blog marketing strategies because they understand the importance of relevant keyword usage and intent

People use the internet for all sorts of things, from reading global news to searching for new opportunities to help their businesses become better. Not all search patterns are organized and consistent. And that's where keyword generation and SEO come out to play.

Implementing Strategies that Work: Become an authority on the topics you blog about

HubSpot is a marketing software, and they are not afraid to stray from their own promotion when it comes to their blog marketing strategies. Most startups use blogs to grab internet users' attention by making sure they closely match the search queries of the prospects.

HubSpot has taken it a step further with exhaustive coverage on topics ranging from *Instagram* Marketing to Resume Building, and sales strategies you need to become successful.

Why are they not sticking to solely promoting their own name? Well, they are a marketing tool themselves, and by blogging about tips on how to build a marketing strategy or conducting marketing research, they are catering to millions of internet queries. This automatically brings all those people to *HubSpot's* website (thanks to their excellent *Google* Rankings), making their platform more popular than any other blog out there.

They have blog series like *Made@HubSpot* and *The Surround Sound Series*, where writers publish articles that indulge readers/subscribers in all sorts of ideas and predictions related to everything between sales and marketing. By covering important topics and highlighting trending keywords, they are building an image as a trustworthy source for information on the vast internet. That gives them the authority on a lot of marketing topics, which drives more people to their website and their platform.

Conclusion: Effective marketing via blogs can be achieved mainly by focusing on what your users want/search for on the internet

When it comes to blogging, there is no formula. But it is

important to build a sense of authority on the internet for people to take your blogs seriously. Marketing strategies that include blogging must ensure they are using the right statistics for effective results.

CHAPTER 3 - SETTING THE GAME PLAN

After completing your research, you'll have all the information needed to kick start your marketing campaign. Now it's time to make a list of tasks, divide them into workable items, allocate work, and see things in action. Being a good marketer has more to do with efficient project management then we normally get credit for. Based on your position and job responsibilities, you'll need to oversee the output of different teams thus, it's critical that you understand the big picture and how different moving parts align with each other.

In the next few lessons, we'll understand the campaign communication basics and make a monthly marketing plan for a popular SaaS product. We'll also see basic tools you can use and common issues that you may run into during execution.

The first step to creating an effective campaign is to have a good central theme. Your theme should point to the benefits of your product and be consistent with the overall business vision (mantra). Hence, it's critical (especially for new ventures) to have clarity on what the company stands for and then accordingly make marketing communication around your theme. Let's dive deeper into the nuances of Business Mantra and how you can craft one for your company.

Business Mantra

When you learn why, how, and what you do, you also understand why, how, and what you won't do. A business mantra communicates what your company does and the idea behind it. You can also refer to it as your mission statement. Your business mantra is what I would call the foundation on which your entire communication strategy is built and evolved. It guides the intent behind every piece of content.

Let's look at the mission statements aka "mantras" of some of the most well-marketed SaaS businesses:

Canva - To empower the world to design

Dropbox - To simplify life for people around the world. Dropbox lets people bring their docs, photos, and videos everywhere and share them easily.

Spotify - To unlock the potential of human creativity—by giving a million creative artists the opportunity to live off their art and billions of fans the opportunity to enjoy and be inspired by it.

Now you can answer:

Why Canva has a design school?

Why Dropbox's homepage says "Say goodbye to busy-work"? and

Why does Spotify have a stellar artist's community?

To craft your own business mantra, I suggest using Simon Sinek's Golden Circle. In his book "Start With Why" the author shares the idea of laying down the foundation of your business with WHY. It has three basic steps:

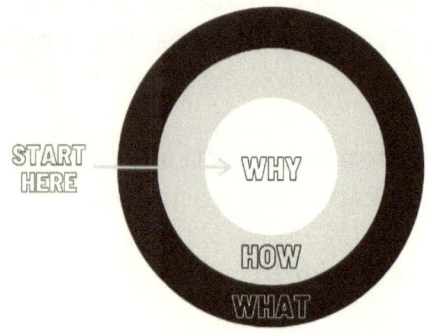

1. Ask yourself why you do what you do. What is it that you care about as a company and what problems you want to solve?
2. Then see how you accomplish your vision. What help or solution you provide to accomplish your company's goal.
3. And finally, what exactly your business can do for the cause.

We can easily observe this framework in our examples and above and in many other ventures. The mantra of Spotify, in particular, is something that you should analyze and then make one for your own company.

Content Plan

Now that you have your mission statement, it's time to expand that one sentence into a brand and for that, you'll need a content plan. Below we'll go through the steps on how to go about making a content plan that really aligns with the brand and delivers results.

Content Audit

A good content plan always starts with an objective study of the content that you have already created. A simple SEO audit followed by keyword research reveals major search terms you are ranking for, your priority areas, low hanging fruits, and areas of long-term growth.

The content audit also involves listing down the topics you have already covered in your blogs so you don't create duplicate content. A simple use case of audit can be understood by comparing the websites of Crello and Canva. Both are exceptional design tools with similar offerings and pricing models, but Canva has been around longer and has a massive library of design-related resources, while Crello mostly has product-centric blogs. Hence, while Canva would focus on growth and expanding on current libraries, Crello would focus on laying the foundation by covering the fundamental areas of design first.

Set Your Goals

Goals not only direct your efforts in the right direction but also serve as a benchmark for performance. The best way to validate whether your goals are appropriate is to follow the "SMART goals with a stretch" approach. We can breakdown SMART as:

S - Specific
M - Measurable
A - Achievable
R - Relevant
T - Time-Based

And the 'stretch' is to make your goals a little higher than attainable. This brings in challenges and makes you push harder towards growth.

Bring in the Research

In the first chapter, we discussed a lot of different ways to dig in data for your company's marketing. It's time to put all that data together and bring out the relevant topics from it:

1. Use SWOT analysis to select topics that cover your weaknesses and highlight your strengths. Take advantage of upcoming trends and inspect the entry of new competitors and any declining trends in keyword volumes.
2. Your competitor may be doing a terrific job, so why not take some hints from what's working for them to outrank them?

3. Your buyer persona and goals will act as filters between the topics you shortlisted and the content that you'll put in the calendar.

Priority Setting - Channel, Type, Frequency

You need to prioritize the type of content you want to create and the ideal placements for them. I recommend setting priorities on 3 levels:

Channel - Choosing the right channel is so critical that we dedicated our second chapter to the subject. Just to reiterate based on your buyer persona, budget, and human resources, choose the channels that will make the biggest impact and are most often used by your prospects.

Content-Type - It's getting more and more important to create content in multiple formats. Blogs can only make the cut for micro-niches now. If you are in a competitive market using infographics, ebooks and videos will help you gain small fractions of audiences from unique sources. While it is helpful to create content in multiple formats, it's also costly and time-consuming. You'll need to create a lot of content to get noticed and will need to stick to them in the long run hence choose the format that fits your resources in the long run.

Frequency - Too little too late is a popular expression in content marketing for a reason. You can rarely go wrong with publishing more content, but less content can easily leave you unnoticed. Hence, try to push content at regular intervals so you see faster results from your campaign without getting lost in the web clutter.

Brainstorming Session

Once you have completed the above steps, you need to list down all the topics that come to your mind and the content format you think would be suitable for them. This brainstorming session aims at bringing a list of powerful and filtered ideas that are meant to go in the content plan.

Making the Calendar

A content and social media calendar combined complete your content marketing plan. I recommend finalizing both the plans together so that your social media team effectively promotes the blogs and is ready with graphics that would go in posts related to the website updates.

Social Media Calendars

We have emphasized time and again on the importance of social media marketing. A calendar helps you keep track of posts, plan for occasions and trends, schedule posts in advance, and synchronize posts with the overall campaign. Let's first see the type of posts that a social media calendar should cover:

1. Blog and Product Posts:

Social media links to blogs and product updates help you bring the audience to your website and create a secondary source of regular traffic. Be sure to keep posting not just your new posts but also your old blog posts on social platforms with the right hashtags.

2. Topical and Seasonal Posts:

We often see a lot of topical content around holidays like Christmas, Halloween, etc. It takes special effort to get noticed during such occasions, and hence social media should plan for them ahead of time.

3. Engagement Posts:

The contests, giveaways, polls, memes, etc. do not bring the audience to your website, but they are an excellent way of getting attention from a mass audience and building a following that you can later leverage. We recommend planning at least one such high-engagement activity every month for B2C solutions and once every quarter for B2B audiences.

The steps to planning a social media calendar are like that of a content calendar. That doesn't come as a surprise, as social media is a part of your overall content plan. Now that we know the content to cover, channels you need to choose and the audience let's see the steps you should take to make a social media calendar:

1. Audit your social networks and make a note of the frequency of posts needed to keep the audience engaged. We suggest below frequency of daily posts for major social media platforms:

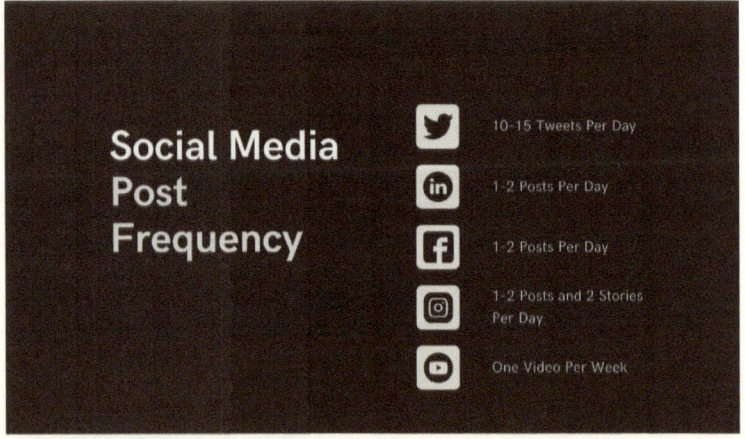

2. Based on your resources, content library, audience and bandwidth choose the social channels that you want to prioritize.

3. Refer to your blog posting schedule and first select slots in the calendar for blog posts promotion followed by top-

ical posts and fill in the remaining with evergreen or engagement based posts.

4. Once the calendar is ready, share it with your team so designers and copywriters know in advance what posts they need to work on so you don't end up lacking assets at the time of posting content.

5. Use a social media scheduling tool like HubSpot, Buffer or Hootsuite etc. to set up posts in advance and measure engagement from multiple platforms under one roof.

Content Plan and Social Calendar for a Design Solution

Throughout this book, we have emphasized on learning from case studies and examples, so let's continue with our approach by designing a content plan for an up-and-coming design solution. For ease of understanding, we can take examples of Crello or Ludus. While both these solutions offer interactive web design solutions, they have distinct features and haven't done a lot of content-based marketing.

We are going to make a one-month content plan and social calendar for a design solution. We can adapt this to any alternative design solution. Let's go step by step:

Content Audit:

As we are starting afresh, we only have blogs about product news and feature announcements. So content audit gives us the idea that we have all the freedom, but also we need to cover the basics and popular keywords in the niche.

Smart Goals:

Before we start, we need a goal in mind. Let's keep it simple for now - a 15% increase in traffic and a 30% increase in *Instagram* followers. We are prioritizing Instagram as that's where artists thrive and we have so much audience and attention to capture.

Ideal Buyer Persona:

For our case, let's consider a social media marketer in a boutique agency as the ideal buyer. They have to create a lot of content for social media, but they rarely have access to expert graphic designers for everyday content needs. They also need to present their achievements and pitches to clients for which they need well-designed presentations.

SELLING THROUGH CONTENT

Creative Jane
Social Media Manager

Identifiers

Age:
22 to 35 years

Education
Bachelor's degree or higer.

Social Networks:
Facebook, Twitter, Instagram

Industry
Advertising

Organization Size:
2-30 Employees

Personal Profile

I am a social media marketing specialist with a knack of finding trends and getting brands noticed in the crowded social media environment.

How to reach out ?

Preferred Method of Communication

- Email
- Face-To-face
- Phone
- Direct Message on Social Media

They Gain Information From

- Business Websites
- Social Media Sites
- Peers
- Facebook Groups

Tools They Need to Do Their Job

- Social Media Analytics Tools
- Social Media Posting Tools
- Productivity Tools (Like Sticky Notes)

Work Life

Job Responsibilities

- Finding New Trends
- Creating Social Media Content
- Managing Brands Presence and Reputation

Goals

- Increase Social Media Engagement and Brand Mentions.

Biggest Challenges

- Regular content creation
- Tracking results

Reports To

- Client
- Account Managers
- Head of Marketing

How does my business address these pain points?

My web app makes it easy for non-designers to create stunning content for social media and presentations with the help of templates.

SWOT Analysis:

Strengths	Weaknesses
Easy to use templates attract novice designers	An expert designer will find such tools limiting
A good share of users gained through guerilla marketing ensures a ready audience for content	Difficult to explain the USP of a product before getting people to actually use the software.
With links flowing from top sites like Product Hunt, Entrepreneur, etc. the backlink profile is solid.	The learning curve associated with a solution may result in users not having a great first experience.

Opportunities	Threats
With more and more design-friendly social platforms, the need for such tools is increasing.	The highly competitive industry with tools like Canva already doing extensive content marketing
Increase in awareness about digital marketing flowing in more and more prospects towards easy-to-use design solutions.	Easy for new tools to get attention from existing users through Facebook groups and comparison websites like G2 Crowd.

We need SWOT analysis to know the angle in which we should gear the content. From basic research we got to know:

- Targeting marketers is a good bet, as they are increasingly looking for such a solution.
- It won't be a good idea to market the product as a replacement for professional design tools be-

cause of its limitations and lack of flexibility.
- Templates are the best way to attract attention, so we need to keep investing in creating more and more templates.
- We need to keep a track of our competitors using a tool like SEMRush to be aware if they start marketing on the same lines as we are.
- Since we already have a good backlink profile, we can target highly competitive keywords and still get ranked in a brief time span.

Keyword Research:

Based on our target persona, I pulled out a keyword list from Google Keyword Planner and shortlisted the below keywords because of their high search volume. We'll use this list to find quality topics for our blog in the brainstorming session.

Keyword	Avg. Monthly Searches
templates for social media posts	880
free Facebook post templates	140
templates for social media posts	880
social media schedule template	390
social media posting calendar	480
social media posting schedule template	140

social media size templates	40
social media banner sizes	260

Priority Setting - Channel, Type, Frequency

Let's put in the starter content plan which I think will most business in this niche:

Focus Channels - Instagram and Website

Content Type - Blogs and Images

Frequency - Daily 2 post on Instagram and 2 weekly blog posts

Putting Things in Calendar:

After we are done setting the guidelines, it's time to brainstorm ideas, and put things in a calendar. Below is how the final out would look like:

Content Schedule [Month]

Publish Date	Due Date	Author	Topic/Title	Keyword(s)
2-Apr-21	1-Apr-21	Yogesh Jain	10 Must-try templates for your social media posts [This Summer]	templates for social media posts
7-Apr-21	6-Apr-21	Amrutha Srivatsa	10 Things you should include in your social media posting calendar	social media posting calendar, social media schedule template
9-Apr-21	8-Apr-21	Yogesh Jain	Our most popular free Facebook post templates in 2020	free Facebook post templates
14-Apr-21	13-Apr-21	Amrutha Srivatsa	Know your social media banner sizes	social media banner sizes, so-

SELLING THROUGH CONTENT

			for 2021 [The Complete Guide]	cial media size templates
16-Apr-21	15-Apr-21	Yogesh Jain	Free *Facebook* post templates for B2B businesses.	free *Facebook* post templates
21-Apr-21	20-Apr-21	Amrutha Srivatsa	The all you need social media calendar template is here [Download]	social media posting calendar, social media schedule template
23-Apr-21	22-Apr-21	Yogesh Jain	9 Design tips when working with social media post templates	templates for social media posts
28-Apr-21	27-Apr-21	Amrutha Srivatsa	Free *Facebook* Post templates for fashion businesses.	free *Facebook* post templates
30-Apr-21	29-Apr-21	Yogesh Jain	Top 10 templates for social media posts straight from the experts	templates for social media posts

Tip - You can include a column for synopsis and target buyer persona for more clarity to the authors.

Social Media Schedule [Week]:

Date	Time [PST]	Message Theme (Final message to be drafted by a copywriter)	Content Type
Monday, 12 April, 2021	10.00.00	Our most popular free Facebook post templates in 2020 (link in bio)	Blog (Promotion)
	20.00.00	Try Crello (Your Design Solution) and share your design ideas with us to win a 30-day premium plan. #CrelloCreation	Engagement (Contest)
Tuesday, 13 April, 2021	10.00.00	Try Crello (Your Design Solution) and share your design ideas with us to win a 30-day premium plan. #CrelloCreation	Engagement (Contest)
	20.00.00	Our most popular free Facebook post	Blog (Promotion)

		templates in 2020 (link in bio)	
Wednesday, 14 April, 2021	10.00.00	Design 101 (Always refer to the color pallette deciding combinations) #WednesdayWisdom	Engagement (Tip)
	20.00.00	10 Things you should include in your social media posting calendar (link in bio)	Blog (Promotion)
Thursday, 15 April, 2021	10.00.00	Get to Know Your Customers Day #GetToKnowYourCustomersDay	Topical (Trend)
	20.00.00	Design Hack 102 (Don't get carried away with fonts) #ThursdayThoughts	Engagement (Tip)
Friday, 16 April, 2021	10.00.00	10 Things you should include in your social media posting calendar (link in bio)	Blog (Promotion)
	20.00.00	National Wear Your Pajamas to Work Day #PJDay	Topical (Trend)
Saturday, 17 April, 2021	10.00.00	10 Must try templates for your social media posts [This Summer] (link in bio)	Blog (Promotion)
	20.00.00	Design Hack 103 (Align your objects well) #instagood	Engagement (Tip)

Tip - You can include a column for a link to the image and final post copy for ease in post scheduling.

Gantt Chart

Calendars are great in planning ahead of time and making sure that the promotion activities are consistent. Marketers though not just have to plan, they need to collect output from specialists like copywriters, designers, developers, and analysts. That's why many softwares are created for us to manage deliverables from different departments and ensure that we maintain the workflow.

Tools like *Trello* and *Asana* allow you to create workflows, allocate tasks, and mark completion or give a review on the output. But if you just need to manage a small team, then a Google sheet will do. It's time we put on our project manager's hat and learn about a popular organizing tool called Gantt chart.

A Gantt is a basic project management tool that helps you divide a task into small deliverables, allocate them to individuals and keep track of each milestone, thus ensuring that things are completed in time. It sounds like a lot, but it really is a simple sheet. Below is a snapshot of what may look like.

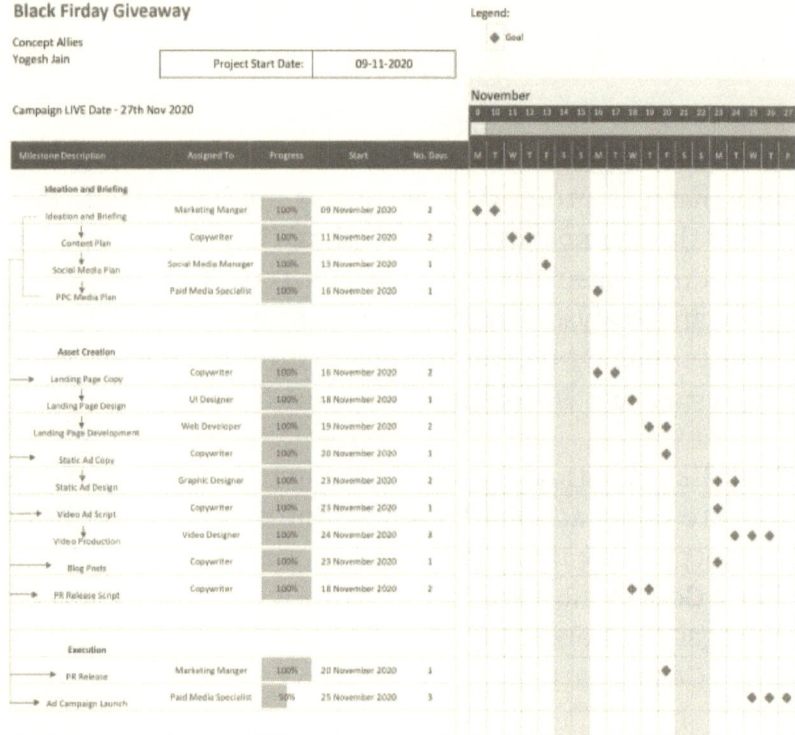

A Gantt Chart has many moving parts. Let's look at the basic 8 elements that make up a Gantt chart:

Task list: A task list is a rundown of tasks that are related to your campaign. You can see the list in the leftmost column of the image above and see how we have grouped the tasks in different heads. It describes the project work in chronological order.

Timeline: Timeline runs horizontally for each task, showing the time required as small diamond symbols. You can observe a calendar view of your tasks with the help of the header row of the timeline section.

Bars: Horizontal markers (diamond symbols) on the right side of the Gantt chart represent tasks on the timeline and show progress, duration, and start and end dates.

Milestones: Some tasks are more critical than others and thus represent an important event in the plan. We can mark these as milestones (represented by flags) to mark an achievement. In our case, we have a tiny Gantt chart, so I avoided marking these to keep it straightforward.

Dependencies: We need to perform certain tasks in a chronological order. For instance, you can't start publishing blogs before making the website and content plan. We can mark such dependencies using lines so it's easy to connect the dots later.

Progress: This shows the percentage of work completed in a progress bar.

Resource assigned: Each task has an accountable individual assigned to it who is suitable and available for the role. In our case, we have marked this area as a job profile for ease of understanding.

A Gantt chart helps you plan work in advance and estimate the time required for the task. Hence, it comes in handy throughout the project (campaign). As marketers, we move into a management role at some point in our career where operational skills like task management come in handy. You should build these skills early in your career, so you are prepared for most of the uncertainties in a project.

Fact: Gantt chart is named after Henry Gantt, but it was originally an idea of Karol Adamiecki who published about it in Harmonogram (since the publication was in Polish he got little exposure).

Managing Common Challenges

A lot of marketing challenges involve thinking on your feet and coming up with solutions on your own. Every business is unique and so should be your solution, but there are some problems that daunt every marketer at some point in their career and we will discuss them in further detail below.

Low Spending Capacity

We have discussed how important it's to have a sizable budget so that you don't get forgotten amidst the hundreds of ads a user sees on a daily basis. That said, some businesses aren't profitable enough or have deep enough pockets to get to that spend and you have to get results nevertheless. When I started my career, I almost exclusively worked on solving this problem at my job as a content marketer. Working for bootstrapped startups means that you'll be facing this challenge for a prolonged period before the business makes enough to spend well on advertising.

I like the approach of divide and rule here. Britishers could rule India for a century with this, we might as well take the hint and start implementing it in business. What I mean is that we divide everything - channels, audience, geographies - and then instead of going big, we go incredibly small. You may not dominate the market of executives in the

NAFTA nations with Facebook and Google search, but sure we can try to make a mark on young executives in Illinois and Texas by dominating LinkedIn.

Clicks Not Leading to Conversions

A common problem with content marketing is the low conversion rate. As we go broad with our topics, the bounce rate increases and the conversion rate decreases. It is an obvious outcome of targeting the top of the funnel audience who may not even have a buying intention, to begin with. For example, if *HubSpot* writes an article on common web-design mistakes, then it may not get conversions from it because a lot of designers will visit the page who neither have the intention nor the required influence for the purchase decision.

I would say that this isn't something we should panic about. It's normal for users to not convert with top of the funnel content. In fact, you aren't supposed to expect conversions from this stage. Here are some things you can do to increase the lead inflow:

1. Create gated content for the top of the funnel audience with short(er) forms to get conversions from people not ready to make a purchase decision.
2. Improve your landing page experience as much as you can. Make sure that the content matches the user's expectations. For instance, if you sell a home antivirus solution, then the user shouldn't land on the 'all products' page, where they have

to find the suitable security solution for their personal laptop.
3. You should always target the right audience by prioritizing long-tail keywords. It's difficult to rank for keyword "security solutions" and you may not get the right audience, but targeting a keyword like "home antivirus software for Windows 10" will give you a quality audience with lower competition.

It's Noisy Out There

Social Media, Google Search, *YouTube* - You name the channel and there will be competitors already doing splendid work with their content marketing. You being a bootstrapped startup have priorities like giving salaries on time and making sure that you at least breakeven if not make enough profit to sustain the business. So how do you make the cut?

The problem is like the budget constraints that we just discussed, bigger fishes don't let small fishes survive for long. The solution is simple; you just have to divide and rule, but sometimes even then your hands are tied. This is where your differentiating factors and market research kicks in. Maybe you aren't able to dominate Google search because of immense competition, but what about the second biggest search platform? No, not Bing. How about *YouTube*? Many businesses don't create enough content for *YouTube*, and that's sad for them and great for you. You should find some areas that your competitors aren't covering well and start making your hold there. As you develop your own fan base, it will be easier to make an entry in competitive keywords because your channel's authority in the domain will increase.

Another way to go about this is by being social for real. Building relations with micro-influencers by distributing free samples, taking part in niche Facebook groups, connecting with posts and activities of LinkedIn members are some ways in which you can build personal relations on social networks. This has a snowball effect on content marketing. As you build relations, you develop a small loyal community of post engagers who support your content and help it reach organically to more users and you do the same in return. Thus, fostering relations instead of turning into a content machine.

These were some generalized solutions that can help any marketer. While the list of challenges and potential solutions can never be conclusive, knowledge of best practices will help you choose the optimal approach faster. With this, I will move to our next lesson on funnel marketing, where you will learn the nuances of content marketing and how it really brings success to businesses.

CHAPTER 4 - ALL HAIL THE FUNNELS

I realized the potential of funnels when I was working as a consultant for Growthplug - a marketing software for clinical practitioners like dentists, paediatrician, etc. As you can guess, all high-value keywords like "dental marketing software", "dental website solutions" etc. were extremely competitive and had low search volume.

Even with paid advertising, we couldn't generate enough leads to keep our sales team productive. Social media channels didn't give quality leads, as that's not the place where doctors spend most of their time. Hence, we were stuck with complaints from both the sales team and the founder with no immediate solution in hand.

We had to capture the prospects even before they were looking for our solution. To counter this, we created an ebook brimming with ideas for all marketing priorities of dentists. Then we created ad campaigns and content to attract dentists to download the ebook. Once a dentist shared the contact details, we sent them emails at regular intervals to inform them about possible automated solutions to their problems, and then we scheduled meetings with them to close the deals.

This is a classic example of funnel marketing where you capture the contact details of a prospect when they are in research mode, send them relevant emails (or show ads) at regular intervals, and then make a sale. You help prospects throughout the buyer's journey (more about it later) and not just start pushing your product through sales calls. The biggest advantage of funnel based marketing is that you establish trust between your brand and prospect so they choose your product while making a purchase decision.

Hence we need to understand the buyer's journey, establish what we need to communicate at different stages, and identify the right channels to communicate. Let's discuss the different stages of the funnel and how we tailor the content for each.

1. Awareness:

At this stage, the prospect is aware of the problem and looking for potential solutions. It is easy to gain visibility here as there are ample search terms that you can consider ranking for. Try to focus on blog topics that go through the pros and cons of each solution (including yours).

In our case, Growthplug wants to target dentists who are looking for a marketing automation platform. They probably have issues like:

- My site isn't performing well
- I am unable to generate enough patient reviews
- I need a way to allow patients to book online appointments and so on.

We can convert these into respective blog topics:

- 10 hacks to improve site speed and ensure maximum uptime
- How to generate reviews from your patients without being nosy?
- How a mobile-friendly online booking system can help your dental practice?

Notice how our first blog topic isn't even tailored to dentists. At the awareness stage, you can afford to have broad topics if they have the potential to bring quality prospects to you.

Channels - Traffic from search engines, social media posts, and click and engagement based ads.

2. Interest:

Once a prospect is aware of your brand (and many times also your competitors) we consider them in the interest stage. At this point, they start engaging with your content on social media and blogs. This is the perfect stage to capture the contact details of your customers using an opt-in form. The prospects trust your brand enough to share contact details and are ready to understand your solution in detail.

We generated the majority of leads for Growthplug at this stage of the customer's journey even though the lead magnets were visible from the very beginning.

Channels - Traffic from search engines and lead generation ad campaigns.

3. Desire:

As a prospect moves to this stage they have narrowed down their search to a handful of options and congratulations if you made it till here. They are aware of your solution but are also knowledgeable about competitors and supplementary solutions. During this stage, you need to steer them in your direction. Communicating about offers, free consultations and differentiating features of your product are some good ways to gain this edge.

In the case of Growthplug, once we acquired the prospect's email address, we started sharing product-related updates once a week to help them make an informed purchase decision.

Channels - Search engine traffic, email marketing, remarketing, and sales-focused campaigns.

4. Action:

Your prospects eventually take action and make a purchase. In the case of a service-based business, this can mean making a small payment for an audit or depositing a token amount. At this point, communication should be product-centric. You can share offers on the product and remove barriers with free trials and follow up for a meeting to help them make a purchase.

Channels - Remarketing ads, email marketing, search engine traffic

5. Advocacy:

An efficient digital marketing funnel never ends with a sale you should either direct the customers to the funnel of a different product or complimentary service. A study by Harvard Business Review proved that acquiring a new customer is up to 25 times more expensive than upselling to existing customers.

Another reason to focus on customer advocacy is to maintain long-term client relations and improve word of mouth. A report by Nielsen showed that as high as 92% of consumers believe suggestions from friends and family more than advertising. You should keep in touch with customers, collect testimonials, and resolve issues at regular intervals.

Channels - Email marketing

Blogging and social media posts excel in getting your brand noticed in the early stages of the buyer's journey, but as your prospects progress through the later stages it gets challenging to remain visible and engage them through organic media. It happens because the level of competition increases and the number of potential keywords reduces at the same time. Hence, you need more than just organic channels to stay on top of your buyers' minds. Email marketing and advertising to engaged audiences play a key role here as they help you get noticed when your prospects are about to make the purchase decision.

ABC of Email Marketing

We have emphasized the importance of email marketing so much that it's imperative that we cover it in detail. It has emerged as one of the foremost ways to enhance brand loyalty and grab customer attention in the SaaS space. Primarily because your customers are working on a laptop all day long, so where better to approach them than via email. Marketing a SaaS product is no cakewalk, as it's harder to showcase the value in a product that doesn't physically exist.

> *"If you are not seeing the email channel as a money-making machine, you have the wrong strategy"*
>
> —Hans Smellinckx (Growth strategist and thought leader)

Email marketing is a powerful tool for SaaS businesses to drive revenue. If that's not working for you, it could be for many reasons. Several SaaS businesses fail to drive conversions with email marketing as they struggle to find qualified leads, design conversion-based emails, or follow-up timely. For others, the problem is as fundamental as not sending emails regularly. To have an email list and not leverage it is a lost opportunity.

Best Email Marketing Practices for Saas Businesses

Your mailing list is precious—you've spent the substantial effort to get it, so you don't want to lose it over methods proven to fail. Audiences are only one click away from unsubscribing, and the reasons are a dime a dozen. Maybe you reach out too often, or your emails seem too driven to make a sale rather than explain how you can solve a problem; whatever may be the reason, failure is one poor strategy away.

Canva's email is catchy, clean, and interesting

Fortunately, there's plenty you can do right as well, especially when you review other's failures and learn how to do better. Let's discuss some of the best practices when executing an email marketing strategy as a SaaS business:

Be human
No one wants to open an email with a subject line in

shouty capitals. Likewise, readers are likely to not take any further action if the email body seems robotic. Make sure your emails always have a human touch.

A good subject line is everything
In most cases, your subject line decides whether the recipient will open your email. If they don't open it, it doesn't matter how effective the content within is. So yes, getting the right subject line for your email is of paramount importance, but make sure you don't get too carried away. Add a catchy and concise subject line without gimmicky effects, such as all capitals or multiple exclamation marks at the end.

> *"On average, five times as many people read the headline as read the body copy. When you have written your headline, you have spent eighty cents out of your dollar."*
>
> — David Ogilvy

Be personal
Today, your lead's inbox has hundreds of emails vying for her attention. You need every edge you can get to stand apart from the crowd. One of the best ways to do this is going one step ahead of being human and getting personal. Use the person's name in the greeting to catch their eye and don't forget to add your signature with a photo or logo at the end.

> *Emails with personalized subject lines generate 50% higher open rates.*

—Yes Lifecycle Marketing, 2017

Segmentation is indispensable

Given personalization is the need of the hour, email segmentation is vital for all marketers. You can use segmentation to cater to potential customers from different industries with specific, targeted messages. Or you can segment your prospects based on whether they're in the free trial period, or they've chosen not to buy the product after the trial.

Follow up, not too much but not too little

Much like any other sales pitch, when to follow up is a pivotal question that could make or break the deal. If you follow up too often, you could be a bother, and if you don't, you may lose potential business. There's no magical number here, it depends on your buyers, your industry, and the product's nature. But testing the results of your previous campaigns to assess what has worked for you can give a good idea for future campaigns.

> *31% of B2B marketers say email newsletters are the best way to nurture leads.*

- Content Marketing Institute, 2020

Don't neglect the CTA, it's the end goal after all

Many marketers end up sending emails that are far too cluttered. There's a bunch of text and a lot of different things going on, and they hide the CTA buttons between all of this. Don't lose sight of the end goal; make sure the CTA buttons are bright and visible and in line with what you mean to convey. Also, add alt text to the buttons and hyperlink them to the landing pages.

Concise body and a clear CTA button in Spotify's email

Understand your buyer persona

One of the foundations of building an effective email marketing campaign is understanding your customers. Who are they? What are their current needs? How can you best reach them? Narrowing down to an accurate buyer persona can help you better direct your marketing efforts.

> *Using buyer personas in email campaigns glean 2x the open rate and 5x the click-through rate*
>
> — <u>The ROI of Buyer Personas</u>, BrightTALK

Timing is key

It's the age of smartphones, and while that's dandy because your email is (most likely) in front of your intended reader as a notification the very minute you hit send, it has its drawbacks too. Customers suffer from email fatigue — a condition where buyers tire from receiving emails — and don't wish to check anything, especially at a busy time. You can follow proven wisdom and pick between Tuesday and Thursday (1–3 pm). But we recommend you experiment to see what day and time works best for your business by assessing how your target audience behaves.

Write what your prospects want to hear and not what you want to say

With the number of emails people receive every day, it's impossible to expect they will open each one. Ensure yours is by appealing to their interest and offering solutions to their challenges rather than merely talking about your product.

How to Make a Good Drip Email Marketing

Campaign?

An email drip marketing campaign is a strategic approach in email marketing proven to better foster connections with leads, enhance revenue, increase retention with regular communication, and reengage lost prospects.

> *Drip email works – generating 3x the click-through rate of a typical marketing email.*
>
> —Martech Zone

In email drip marketing, we automatically send a series of preset emails to target subscribers (prospects/customers) at pre-defined time intervals or when they complete a milestone task. For instance, you could set up a campaign where a prospect would receive the first email upon sign up, the second two days later, and the third when they visit your website again. Such a campaign enables you to personalize messages fin bulk based on an action.

> *Companies that excel at drip marketing generate 80% more sales at 33% lower costs.*
>
> —Martech Zone

Drip emails are crucial as they help you foster relationships. Let's say a prospect has just signed up for your newsletter, you (of course) will send them an email, but you don't want to leave it there. Consistently emailing them after set periods will help you build a relationship that you can leverage later. And the best part is, despite being an automated process, you can personalize these emails with the subscriber's name and company info, with consideration to their behavior. Remember, in such a campaign we must meticulously plan each email and its sequence to drive a specific action.

You can set up email drip campaigns for:

- Interesting and informative updates
- Release updates
- Invoices
- Holiday campaigns
- Subscription notices and more.

Many marketing agencies can set up an email drip marketing campaign for you, but you can get one up and running yourself as well. Let's review the steps involved in building a good drip email marketing campaign.

Step 1: Identify and segment your target market

Much like in any other marketing efforts, identifying your target market is the first step in building an effective drip email marketing campaign. You first need to consider:

- Who your target customers are
- What topics they are interested in
- Which keywords they use while searching for products similar to yours
- How they compare products
- What the key considerations are in the final purchase decision

- What problem does your product solve for these prospects

As a SaaS company, you could create multiple buyer personas, depending on the product categories and pricing. Further, you want to segment your target market to set campaigns as per each segment's needs. Your target group could be people who have downloaded your app or signed up for a free trial.

Step 2: Define what you hope to achieve with the campaign

Again, similar to other marketing approaches, you need to define the aim for your drip email marketing campaign. Not only will this help steer all your efforts in the right direction, but it will also help you measure your campaign's performance. Here are some examples of campaign objectives:

- Lead nurturing
- Onboarding
- Upselling or cross-selling
- Improving customer experience

Set 3: Set the trigger

Once you've defined your target market and aim, you can set up the trigger, which means your email will be sent to the subscriber when they complete a specific action, such as:

- submit into a form on your site

- Visit a specific webpage
- Click a link in an email

Set 4: Draft your emails

Once you've decided which actions will trigger emails, it's time to draft them. Three factors are key when creating emails for drip email marketing; your emails must be:

- Value-adding
- Coherent
- Independent

The first one is a no-brainer—your email must have great content; otherwise, none of this will amount to much. Drafting these emails is a mix of marketing and content writing, as no one truly 'reads' your emails so much as 'scans' them. You want short chunks of text with crisp sub-headings and important information highlighted for easy perusal.

In terms of what to write, provide information that brings the reader one step closer to the action you desire. For instance, if you want more people to use your product, provide information on product features, and add case studies and testimonials that underline how your product helped a customer.

The other two points — coherent and independent — are more specific to email drip marketing. Each email must build on the previous one and belong to the entire campaign, and it must independently appeal to your subscribers. You can create a visual workflow to understand the order and logical progression.

Step 5: Set the timing and frequency

Once everything else is in place, you only need to decide when and how often you will send these emails. It sounds fairly simple but can be tricky. As we discussed in the previous section, there's no guarantee on which days and times work best, so the ideal approach is to experiment and find what works for you. A starting point can be reviewing your newsletter statistics to see if a specific day and time record a higher opening rate. In terms of how often, you want to start with a higher frequency and gradually reduce it with time, from maybe a few times a week to once a week and so on.

Step VI: Measure and optimize

Once you've set up the campaign, it will work on its own with little to no effort on your part. But like with all marketing campaigns, you need to assess the campaign performance to understand what is working and what isn't.

What to measure?
- Open rates and clicks
- Impact on revenue
- Clicks on landing pages

This step is crucial, as it will help you optimize your campaigns to make sure each one is working. If an email isn't performing, you can rewrite the content and AB test different subject lines. Review your campaign's performance once a week as a best practice.

Now that we have learned the process, it's time to see how to put them into action. Below is how a drip-email campaign would look for a musician selling guitar courses online.

Medium	Timing	Subject	Objective
Website		Day 1 - Lead shares email to download the free ebook	
Email 1	Immediate	Here is your free guitar toolkit	Shares a brief about the instructor
Email 2	Day 3	Why choose to learn the guitar the hard way?	Inform about your online guitar course
Email 3	Day 5	You should try this insane guitar lick	Engage users and showcase your skill
Email 4	Day 7	Searching Youtube for the next guitar trick?	Convince that you are better than free options
Email 5	Day 9	I'll make it easy for you to enroll in my course	Give them a free trial or discount
Email 6	Day 11	Last chance to grab the free trial. (Offer ends tomorrow)	Add scarcity to the offer and close deals

Let's look at one more example, this time for a digital marketing software designed for independent gyms and fitness centers.

Medium	Timing	Subject	Objective
Website		Day 1 - Lead shares email to download the free ebook	
Email 1	Immediate	Here is your free business toolkit	Share a brief about the software
Email 2	Day 3	You are not alone in this, technology is with you	Tell about the automated marketing solution
Email 3	Day 5	Zumba vs Tabata - How to choose the right product to promote	Engage users and inform so they trust you
Email 4	Day 7	Your website should bring in more members	Share about your website solution
Email 5	Day 9	No renewals can be deadly ask them at the right time	Explain the email marketing features
Email 6	Day 11	We will make your website for free (no hidden charges)	Onboard customer for a free month
Email 7	Day 13	Last chance to grab the free offer	Add scarcity to the offer and close deals

Notice how each time we add an email just to re-engage leads and don't come out as too salesy at the beginning of the campaign. For ease of understanding, I have kept this drip campaign very straightforward. As you progress and collect data, you can add a lot more conditions to the workflow.

Lead Scoring

So far we checked how businesses can generate and nurture leads through content marketing. But as businesses mature, the flow of leads becomes overwhelming and the sales team finds it hard to differentiate between people who are buying and those who are just looking around. This is where lead scoring comes in handy.

Lead scoring refers to assigning your leads a value showing sales 'readiness' based on their interest in your products and where they are in the buying cycle. You can have different values as per your preference, or go with the traditional hot, warm, and cold labeling with 'hot' being ready to buy, 'warm' being may consider your product, and 'cold' referring to the leads who aren't ready to make any purchase decision. Lead scoring is important as it helps you understand the action required for each lead, such as whether you need to nurture a certain lead or aggressively target it for sales. Thus, with a good lead scoring model, your sales team can channelize its efforts toward the leads that are most likely to convert.

> *In a study of ten B2B organizations using lead scoring systems, Eloqua found that, on average, deal close rates increased by 30%, company revenue increased by 18%, and the revenue per deal increased by 17%.*
>
> — The Business Case for Integrated Demand Generation whitepaper, Eloqua

Benefits of Lead Scoring

1. Higher sales efficiency
2. Higher marketing effectiveness
3. Better marketing and sale coordination

How Lead Scoring Works

1. Each action (specific page views, site search, download, link clicks, etc.) is assigned points as per its weightage
2. Every action a lead takes earns them points
3. Depending on how many points a lead has, we classify it as hot or cold (or whichever other values you assign)

Is lead Scoring Ideal for Your Business?

1. You have a detailed buyer persona in place
2. You have defined marketing channels and campaigns in line with pricing models
3. You have an efficient sales team in place
4. You have a Martech system (like HubSpot or Marketo) that can track leads and assigning scores once you define the process.

Making a Lead Scoring Model

Ever played Scrabble? Each tile carries some points, and you get awarded based on the word and its position on the board. When we think of a lead scoring model we do something similar, we determine the number of points relevant for each action of the lead and also place an architecture to allocate those points at an appropriate time. Don't worry though, it is much easier to execute than it sounds. Let's see some ways to allocate points and when they should we should use them.

1. Demographic Information

Does your business target a specific demographic like young adults, the elder population, or only females? If yes, you can include relevant fields like 'gender' and 'date of birth' in the forms. So that way you can allocate more points to leads that match your target persona.

You can also subtract points from the leads if they are not the right fit. For example, reducing 10 points from anyone who is from a developing country when you are only targeting first world countries.

Below is a lead scoring model that allocates points based on the age group of the lead. It would be relevant for businesses that have a product for young adults.

- +100 points for 18-25
- +50 points for 25-35
- +10 points for 35-40
- -10 points for 40+

2. Company Information

A B2B organization targeting large-scale enterprises needs business emails of leaders. They would also prioritize a certain size, type, or industry of business. In such cases, it is helpful to score leads on the target market fit.

You ask questions like job role, company size, and industry and allocate more points to leads that fit your target criteria. Here is how a lead scoring model (based on team size) will look for a company targeting mid-size business:

- +0 points for 1-10 employees
- +10 points for 10-50 employees
- +70 points for 50-250 employees
- +50 points for 200-500 employees
- +30 points for 500-1000 employees
- +10 points for 1000+ employees

Note - Notice how the points are higher for the companies with 50 to 250 employees, as that is the preferred target segment.

Software like *HubSpot* can automatically identify company information from a business email so you can also use that data to make such decisions instead of asking everything in the form.

3. Online Behavior

We once experimented with our ad campaigns where we created two remarketing audiences, one of all website visitors and one of the website visitors who had at least two sessions on the website (both for 30 days). As you would expect, the audience that targeted only engaged visitors worked phenomenally better.

Leads that interact with your website and social media pages tend to be already influenced by your brand or are further down the customer journey than those who just came to look around on your site and left. Analyze your past sales data to see if you find any such patterns like more number of sessions before purchase, higher click-throughs from social media sites, time on high-value pages (like pricing, demo request, or features), download of certain collaterals that represent higher sales intent, etc.

On the contrary, you can also give negative scores to the leads who stopped engaging with the website or visited a careers page. Below is a sample points structure based on online behavior:

- +3 points for spending over 1 minute on a blog post
- +3 points for click through from a social media site
- +5 points for downloading a case study or visiting a related page
- +10 points for filling a demo request form
- -50 points for visiting your careers page or filling a job application

4. Email Engagement

We are so used to sharing our email address for gated content that it is no more is an indicator that someone is interested in buying from you unless it's through a demo or contact page. Open and click-through rates on the other hand showcase higher levels of interest in the product.

Not all emails are the same, promotional emails showcase higher purchase intent than routine industry updates. So we should accordingly create a scoring system, like the one below.

- +5 points for opening a newsletter email
- +10 points for clicking through a newsletter email
- +15 points for opening an email related to product updates
- +15 points for clicking through an email related to product updates
- +25 points for opening a promotional email (like limited period offers)
- +35 points for clicking through a promotional email
- -10 for no opens on 3 consecutive emails

While these lead scoring models have their ideal usage, it's beneficial to combine multiple types of lead scoring models and see the score as a collective figure. You can also create two lead scoring models and compare the score to see through which you end up with more relevant leads for your business.

68% of B2B marketers are employing both behavioral and demographic scoring.

—Survey Report: The State of Marketing Automation Maturity, Spear Marketing Group

A common issue that arises is that marketers don't understand which factors are the most important and how to set lead score benchmarks that qualify a lead as cold, warm, or hot. The answers to both lie with the sales team. They engage with the client directly hence, their insight is critical to a successful implementation of a lead scoring system.

Best Practices on Lead Scoring

1. Use a score reduction model, so your scores are not inaccurately inflated
2. Use different lead scoring models for different products
3. Lay emphasis on how you score each action—not all have the same weightage
4. Keep tweaking the model as there is always scope to add additional elements and optimize the existing ones. This is not a do-and-forget activity, but an ongoing process.

Role of PPC in Funnel Marketing

Contrary to popular belief, content marketing is not the same as inbound marketing. Inbound marketing implies that you'll generate all the leads using organic methods like SEO, *YouTube* videos, and social media posts alone. On the other hand, content marketing employs accelerators like advertising to ensure faster results.

I have been handling budgets of over $200,000 since 2019 with the Growth Marketing Team (a performance advertising agency). Working with clients like *Evercoach (by Mindvalley)*, *Scott's Bass Lessons* and *Eden Energy Medicine* made me aware of the impact of advertising on the funnel. Each of them uses advertising to generate enormous volumes of leads, which then convert with the help of remarketing and email marketing.

Advertising itself is a vast field, and hence going around all the tricks of the trade will need another volume from me. Hence I'll just take you through some strategic basics that are worth considering.

1. Get Your Funnels Ready First

You should already have a content flow - emails, landing pages, product demos, blogs - these should be ready before you advertise. Once you put dollars at play, a broken funnel will only burn a hole in your wallet.

Suppose if you generate leads without a functioning way

to nurture them. By the time you make a functioning system, all the leads generated by then would forget about your business and you'll end up with no revenue at hand.

2. Test Organically As Much as Possible

Unless you are in a rush, it's advisable to test your funnels with organic traffic first. Test different landing pages and CTA's using sophisticated tools like *HubSpot* to refine your funnel before advertising it. If you can convert your organic traffic with ease, then you'll surely be able to scale revenue with advertising.

3. Start Small

One of the biggest mistakes I see in advertising is that either people start too small or too big. You need your skin in the game but that doesn't mean that you put all your money on fire.

For instance, I have observed that a lead in the online education space cost between $1.5 to $2. Assuming a decent conversion rate of 2% you'll need at least 50 leads to get one sale. Hence we request clients to spend $500-$800 and see results from that data before going ahead. If you don't generate sales, that means you are doing something wrong. Fix it and try again, but with a slightly lower budget of $500 to cut your losses.

Your funnels will never be perfect, but that's the beauty of marketing. The key is not to wait for perfection, but to strive for it. Keep testing and trying new communication styles and eventually, you'll hit the bullseye i.e. a scalable funnel that helps your business grow exponentially.

AFTERWORD

Marketing as we know it is a lot of art than just a science of principles and know-how. I wrote this book based on the best practices I discovered and studied. I would recommend that you follow these but also keep experimenting with new ideas.

What is the recommended approach today may become an obsolete method tomorrow. For example, keyword stuffing in content was once the best way to rank on the first page of Google. It became so popular that people started writing keywords in white text on blogs so that search engines read it, but they don't affect the user experience. Google soon caught up and started penalizing such sites.

I suggest that you take an audience-first approach with your marketing and concentrate on delivering concrete value. You do that and the business will grow. I hope this book was worth your time, and you got to learn a lot from it.

Please drop a review if you liked it.